POWER
AND
POVERTY
IN THE
CHURCH

POWER
AND
POVERTY
IN THE
CHURCH

*The Renewal and
Understanding of Service*

YVES CONGAR, OP

Paulist Press
New York / Mahwah, NJ

Cover image (background) by HorenkO/Shutterstock.com
Cover design by Tamian Wood
Book design by Lynn Else

This book was first published in France by Les Editions du Cerf, under the title *Pour une Eglise Servante et Pauvre*. First English-language edition, 1964, Geoffrey Chapman Ltd. Translated by Jennifer Nicholson.

Nihil Obstat: Joannes M. T. Barton, STD, LSS, Censor Deputatus

Imprimatur: George L. Craven, Titular Bishop of Sebastopolis in Armenia, Vic. Gen. of Westminster, May 1, 1964

The Nihil Obstat and Imprimatur are a declaration that a book or pamphlet is considered to be free from doctrinal or moral error. It is not implied that those who have granted the Nihil Obstat and Imprimatur agree with the contents, opinions, or statements expressed.

Library of Congress Cataloging-in-Publication Data

Names: Congar, Yves, 1904–1995, author.
Title: Power and poverty in the church : the renewal and understanding of service / Yves Congar.
Other titles: Pour une Eglise servante et pauvre. English
Description: New York : Paulist Press, 2016. | Includes bibliographical references.
Identifiers: LCCN 2016011167 (print) | LCCN 2016023597 (ebook) | ISBN 9780809153039 (pbk. : alk. paper) | ISBN 9781587686382 (Ebook)
Subjects: LCSH: Catholic Church—Government. | Church—Authority.
Classification: LCC BX1802 .C613 2016 (print) | LCC BX1802 (ebook) | DDC 262/.122—dc23
LC record available at https://lccn.loc.gov/2016011167

ISBN 978-0-8091-5303-9 (paperback)
ISBN 978-1-58768-638-2 (e-book)

Published by Paulist Press
997 Macarthur Boulevard
Mahwah, New Jersey 07430
www.paulistpress.com

Printed and bound in the
United States of America

To his Eminence Cardinal Lercaro,
Archbishop of Bologna,
who has made himself the spokesman for the
Church of the Poor: in respectful and filial homage

CONTENTS

PREFACE

How has the Catholic hierarchy lived the ideal of service it received as law from the Lord and the Apostles through the centuries? The obvious continuity of the hierarchical institution shows the mark of time: like houses and their furnishings, it has gone through various styles. The Church has largely been the history, but history has partially determined her characteristics.

I would not have dared tackle it in itself, not because I had nothing to say on the subject but because I am too well aware of my inadequacy. All I hoped to do was to offer a contribution, however indirect and remote, within the limits of my competence, to the study of the ideological causes underlying certain modes of behavior or a certain state of things, which history has conditioned to some extent. It is a fact that at a time when the whole "mystique" of the Church stresses love of the poor and even of poverty, when the Church is truly poor, even sometimes in real need almost everywhere, yet she has the appearance of wealth, and (in a word) of privilege, or has pretensions in that direction. This harms both herself and the cause for whose service she was made and which she truly does desire to serve. How has this regrettable appearance come about?

We would have to study many other aspects in the light of both history and theology to throw light on the problems thus raised, which many find disturbing and even distressing. What is needed is a history and a theology of the Church's temporal state. There are a number of very suggestive studies on this point, but a great deal remains to be said. To what extent can and should the Church apply to herself the gospel requirements that tend to be demanded of individual Christians — forgiveness of enemies, turning the other cheek, choosing the ways of poverty, meeting the temptations of the spirit of possession and power, waging war against the flesh, and so on? Many other questions would still need to be considered.

I believe history is required for their successful treatment. History is a great teacher of truth, especially if by it we mean something more than mere erudition, profitable as this is. What is wanted is an awareness, in full knowledge of the facts, of the historical dimension that affects everything that exists in this world. We are apt to see not only the mystery of the Church, but all ecclesiastical realities (hierarchy, sacraments, and so on), as if they transcend time. That is one of the reasons why we find it so difficult to try to imagine new forms, a new style, for these sacred realities; sometimes we even dismiss the attempt as presumptuous and idle. The episcopate, for example, is an institution of divine and apostolic origin, but historically it has taken more than one form, and it has been lived in very different styles. Because the episcopate, as authority and as sacrament, is always the same, we are inclined to overlook the gulf that separates the leader of a local community in the early Church, a bishop of feudal times, and a twentieth-century pastor. The Church and the priesthood are of all times, but they are also the Church of today, the priesthood of today. Through familiarity with historical forms, we can distinguish more clearly the permanence of the essential and the variation of forms; we can locate the absolute and the relative more exactly, and so remain truer to the absolute while we shape the relative to the needs of the time.

I

THE HIERARCHY AS SERVICE

SCRIPTURAL SOURCES AND HISTORICAL DEVELOPMENT

INTRODUCTORY NOTE

The notion that the hierarchy consists essentially in service is a theme that runs all through Christian tradition. Whether in phrases that have become genuine topoi, type-formulae of ecclesiastical literature, such as *praesse, prodesse* (to be at the head, at the service, of); or in what the Germans call *Devotionsformeln*, titles or style—clauses such as *Servus servorum Dei* (servant of the servants of God);[1] or in the ideology of service for the common good, the good of each and all, contained in the constantly recurring words *utilis, utilitas*; or in ordination sermons like the fine discourses of St. Augustine;[2] or again in the vocabulary introduced by him and still in general use, which distinguishes between the *potestas*, "the authority," of Christ and the pure *ministerium*, or service, of the Church; or finally in treatises more or less expressly devoted to the duties of those vested with authority[3]— the theme is endlessly affirmed, from the New Testament down to the present day.

We shall go first to the New Testament to see what specific conception of authority Jesus handed down to his disciples and how the apostles understood it. For it is on that level that we as Christians must seek to understand and to be "transformed by the renewing of your minds" to the mind of our Master (Rom 12:2; cf. Eph 4:23). Then we shall sketch in the history of authority in the life and thought of the Church, and finally propound a synthesis and interpretation on general lines.

1

TEXTS FROM THE GOSPELS AND REFERENCES IN NEW TESTAMENT LITERATURE

Our Lord spoke with exceptional exactness and emphasis on the subject of service. He did so on three occasions. The third was during the celebration of the Last Supper (St. John is our witness here, at Luke 22:24–27); the first two were at definite and very important moments in his evangelic ministry; our information comes from the Synoptics.

THE QUESTION OF PRECEDENCE

Jesus' preaching in Galilee met with some success among the people. But he knew that the time was come for him to fulfil another chapter in what was written of him; he had to "go up" to Jerusalem, be rejected by the elders and by the high priests and the scribes, suffer many things, and enter on his passover of death and resurrection (see Mark 8:31–33; Matt 16:21–23). Jesus and his disciples were living the brief moment between his preaching in Galilee and the drama that was even then gathering in Judea. Jesus went to Syro-Phoenicia and to Syria itself, to Caesarea Philippi. It was there and at that time (see Matt 16:13ff.) that

Peter's confession of faith, and the first institution, in him, of the new ministry to serve the new justice (the "keys of the kingdom of heaven") took place. Knowing that he was going to his death, Jesus made provision for his work to continue in the person of his apostles. From that time on, says St. Matthew (16:21), Jesus set before the disciples the prospect of the passion, which was at the same time and by implication the prospect of the evangelical ministry, or of "following" in the work of the holy gospel (Matt 16:24–28; Mark 8:32–38).

In Judaism, the right to first place was a matter for endless argument: in gatherings for worship, in administration, at meals, the question of precedence constantly arose. Perhaps in consequence of the promise of the keys of the kingdom to Peter, the other disciples fell to disputing "who was the greatest" (Mark 9:34; cf. Luke 9:46; Matthew, who removes the episode from Caesarea Philippi, says, "the greatest in the kingdom of heaven," 18:1). Jesus answered them by both word and deed; he called a little child into their midst, put his arm round him, and said, "Whoever becomes humble like this child is the greatest in the kingdom of heaven" (Matt 18:4). He went on to explain: should the apostles be received as great, in their capacity as apostles and because of their ministry, it would have nothing to do with any greatness of their own, but would be because of Jesus himself, because of his name. Even a little child bears this same honor if he is received because of Jesus. Jesus himself has this honor only because of the mission he received from his Father. The Father alone is the principle without a source. All comes from him; all is called to return to him.

We must turn to St. John for further development of our Lord's meaning. We shall find there Jesus' infinitely far-reaching statements on his glory—the glory that he has given his disciples, too (John 17:22). This is not the glory of a reputation that exalts us in the eyes of men but a glory that Jesus has from the Father, by virtue of the fact that he reveals both the condescension and the power of the Father, because he knows no other aim in life than to obey the Father's will and accomplish the design for which the Father sent him.[4] That is why Jesus begins to manifest his glory when he begins his ministry (John 2:11). That is why he recognizes and proclaims the special time of his glorification, more than any other time, as the beginning of his passion, which clearly cannot be separated from the resurrection that followed it.[5] This is the supreme moment of his obedience to the Father who sent him to seek, amid the dust and thorns, that which was lost.

In this mission, Jesus is filled with the power of God; the Father has given all things into his hand (John 3:35).[6] "You call me Teacher and Lord—and you are right, for that is what I am" (John 13:13). Jesus' authority with regard to the world and men is absolute, but it is an authority (1) wholly directed to their salvation, by the path of the deepest humiliation and (2) wholly received from the Father, depending on him, and constantly referred to him by Jesus' acknowledgment that he has nothing save from the Father: Jesus' doctrine is not *his* doctrine, his judgment is not *his* judgment (cf. John 7:16; 5:30; 12:49, etc).

WHO SHALL HAVE FIRST PLACE?

In the second episode, Jesus has again announced, "We are going up to Jerusalem" (Mark 10:33), and intimated that his messiahship is now to be decisively affirmed. James and John (Mark 10:35) or their mother (Matt 20:20), come up to him with a direct, outright request that must have been in their minds for some time—that in the kingdom which Jesus is obviously about to establish, they shall receive the two first and best places, and sit one on his right hand and the other on his left. Then the Lord gives a most definitely worded answer:

> You know that among the Gentiles those whom they recognize as their rulers lord it over them, and their great ones are tyrants over them. But it is not so among you; but whoever wishes to become great among you must be your servant, and whoever wishes to be first among you must be slave of all. For the Son of Man came not to be served but to serve, and to give his life a ransom for many. (Mark 10:42–45; cf. Matt 20:25–28)

He uses terms of great force. In the gospel order, as in the order of earthly societies, the great and the first do exist. In earthly societies, they make their power felt, they bear themselves as masters;[7] the whole relationship of inequality between others and themselves is a relationship of subjection on the one hand, of mastery on the other. The path that, according to the gospel, leads to the rank of *first* or *great* is quite different, even the exact opposite. It lies in seeking a situation or relationship not of power but of service, of *diakonos*, "servant," or *doulos*, "slave, common worker." These two terms lie at the very heart of the categories that serve to define Christian existence. *Diakonia*—ministry, the position, behavior, and activity of a servant—appears throughout the whole of the New Testament to be as it were coextensive and practically identical with the character of disciple—a man possessed by Christ and living in subjection to him. The title *doulos*, "slave, servant (of God)," which had no religious significance in the pagan world, best expresses this complete belonging to Christ, in which we become also the servants of all our brothers. The attitude of service, not of power, which Jesus makes his disciples' law, he expressly links with his own—the masters—for the disciple is not merely a pupil under instruction; he imitates the master and shares his life. Jesus lived his mission, and defined it in terms of the Isaian Servant.[8] He came not to "domineer," not to exact service, but to serve as a slave and even to live as a slave, to the point of actually being sold, of letting himself be the equivalent of a ransom.[9] Because their life belongs wholly to Christ, is wholly of him and for him, the disciples can rise only by humbling themselves, only by following Christ on the downward path of self-giving and self-abnegation, along which St. Paul has traced God's victorious trajectory to the death of the cross and from the tomb to glory.

FROM THE FORM OF GOD TO THE FORM OF A SERVANT

The wonderful passage of Philippians 2:6–11, which may have been a Christian hymn, must be read in the same light as the sayings we have already quoted: the way of the flesh is opposed to the way of the spirit, the way of the world to the way of the gospel:

> [Christ Jesus], who, though he was in the form of God,
> did not regard equality with God
> as something to be exploited,

but emptied himself,
    taking the form of a slave,
    being born in human likeness.
And being found in human form,
    he humbled himself
    and became obedient to the point of death—
    even death on a cross.

Therefore God also highly exalted him
    and gave him the name
    that is above every name,
so that at the name of Jesus
    every knee should bend,
    in heaven and on earth and under the earth,
and every tongue should confess
    that Jesus Christ is Lord,
    to the glory of God the Father.

The text speaks only of Christ, but exegetes in general agree in seeing here an allusion to the first Adam, from whom our carnal man proceeds. Although existing in the form of man, that is, as creature and servant, Adam desired and still does desire to enjoy a form of God, which he understands as independence and self-affirmation limited by nothing and no one: "You will be like God, knowing [that is, yourselves determining] good and evil" (Gen 3:5, 22). But desiring to be as God, Adam descended into a state of nakedness (Gen 3:11), a life of toil and attachment to the senses. Man is never his own master; he is always under domination. If he breaks away from the domination of God, he falls under the domination of the "Powers." But though Christ existed in the form of God, he did not bear himself possessively; he did not cling to the divine form as men cling to a prize; he took on himself the form of a slave, our form. Even in this form in which, being God, he could *by right* have claimed to reign supreme over the world, he did not demand his right possessively, he did not snatch it or lay covetous claim to it; he was pleased to obtain it from God by humble, crucifying service, abasing himself in the spirit of love. That is why, while Adam fell through his desire to exalt himself, Christ received the name above all names, the name of the First absolutely, the name of "Lord," at which every knee bows on earth, in heaven, and in hell. "All who exalt themselves will be humbled, and all who humble themselves will be exalted" (Matt 23:12 and parallels—read from v. 8; Luke 14:11; 18:14; 2:48–52).

THE WAY OF LOVE IN HUMILITY AND SERVICE

The "first" man within us longs to dominate, to play the master. Christ came as the "second Adam" or as St. Paul says, the "last Adam," the final Adam, the eschatological man (*eschatos Adam*: 1 Cor 15:45), not a man of domination, but a man of obedience, giving thanks, a man in communion with others, complying with others, or rather complying and communing with God in them, a man of God, who is "all in all" (1 Cor 15:28). The first Adam has life, "became a living being" (Gen 2:7; 1 Cor 15:45). He lives but his life constantly wastes away and renews itself by devouring, that is, destroying, other creatures, appropriating them to itself. But normal life, *true* life, should not be sustained by bringing death. Life should come from within and communicate life. "The last Adam became a life-giving spirit" (1 Cor 15:45). He rediscovers the logic of the spirit, which is not to feed on what it brings in to itself from without and destroys but to shine out from within. This can be achieved only when the order of obedience is perfectly fulfilled,[10] when everything is brought back to its Principle, when "God" is "all in all." It will be, it is, achieved *by Christ*: "As all die in Adam, so all will be made alive in Christ" (1 Cor 15:22). But Christ will achieve this in the end only because he has been like this from the beginning of his mortal life in the flesh. The way resembles its end, and only thus can it lead to its end (see John 14:1–11). The Father is already in Jesus. The way leading to God, who is "all in all," leading, that is, to mankind in communion, is a state where others are not destroyed to sustain life, but where life, coming from God, shines out on all men. It is the way of love in humble service. "For you were called to freedom, brothers and sisters; only do not use your freedom as an opportunity for self-indulgence, but through love become slaves to one another. For the whole law is summed up in a single commandment, 'You shall love your neighbor as yourself.' If, however, you bite and devour one another, take care that you are not consumed by one another" (Gal 5:13–15); all the rest of the chapter should be read in this light. The spirit of possessiveness destroys; *agape*, "love," which is poured forth within us by the Holy Spirit (Rom 5:5), shines forth and edifies (1 Cor 8:1 and the whole of chapter 13).

Such is the way of Christ. Such is first of all the way of "God," that is, of the Father: "Therefore be imitators of God, as beloved children, and live in love [*agape*], as Christ loved us and gave himself up for us" (Eph 5:1–2; and cf. 25). Holy Scripture leaves us in no doubt that the impulse of humble, serving, self-sacrificing love begins in "God," that is, in the bosom of the Father. "In Christ God was reconciling the world to himself" (2 Cor 5:19; cf. John 3:16; 1 John 4:10). The "self-annihilation" of the Son follows the Father's stripping of himself. If Jesus reveals the Father ("Philip, whoever has seen me has seen the Father"), we can go so far as to say that he reveals in the Father a possibility of grace, even a disposition toward *being* Grace, and so coming to us, stooping down to us, humbling himself: because he *is* Love. We should not be talking of the God we know in Jesus Christ if we stopped short at the idea that he is the "Prime Mover, himself unmoved" (Aristotle), or that he is the one who loves himself (Plotinus). In Jesus Christ, God has revealed himself leaning toward us, bending over us, the Love-Gift, Grace.

"IF I HAVE WASHED YOUR FEET…"

We come to know the Father through what is supremely manifested in the attitude of the Son, *come down from heaven* (John 1:18; 3:11 and 16; 14:1–11; 17:6):

> After he had washed their feet, had put on his robe, and had returned to the table, he said to them, "Do you know what I have done to you? You call me Teacher and Lord—

11

and you are right, for that is what I am. So if I, your Lord and Teacher, have washed your feet, you also ought to wash one another's feet. For I have set you an example, that you also should do as I have done to you. Very truly, I tell you, servants are not greater than their master, nor are messengers greater than the one who sent them. If you know these things, you are blessed if you do them." (John 13:12–17)

The Lord's order here—we might almost say, his ordination—comes in the long series of passages in which St. John's Gospel expresses the idea of mission flowing, as it were cascading, from the Father to the incarnate Son and from the incarnate Son to the apostles and the Church.[11] God's design is in fact to communicate himself (see 1 John 3:1–3). For this, the reality on high must exist here below, through successive stages, in a form that shares its virtue though never in full and sovereign measure, and mirrors the behavior of its source and reality. The Father has sanctified the Son and sent him to the world (John 10:36). The Son in turn has sanctified and purified the apostles, and consecrates them by sending them to the world (see John 17:14, 17–19). This is the moment of their consecration. The Synoptic Gospels give us the account of the institution of the Eucharist at this point. St. John omits it, substituting the washing of feet, which he alone reports. Corresponding to "Do this in remembrance of me," we have here, "For I have set you an example, that you also should do as I have done to you." The ordination of the apostles is an ordination in terms of service. Christ, who washes the disciples' feet and speaks of his action in this way, is the same Christ who knows that the Father has given all things into his hands (13:3) and who expressly recalls his character of Master and Lord, *Didaskalos* and *Kurios*, just as he refers to his *exousia*, his power, at his final sending of the apostles (Matt 28:18). At this supreme moment of the Last Supper, he repeats his essential teaching: his disciples, and most especially Simon Peter, are to follow him in serving one another:

The kings of the Gentiles lord it over them; and those in authority over them are called benefactors. But not so with you; rather the greatest among you must become like the youngest, and the leader like one who serves. (Luke 22:25–26)

"OURSELVES YOUR SLAVES!"

We find the echo of the Master's teaching in the apostles themselves. The first Christian texts are probably St. Paul's. Paul took to himself, as though by right, the character of *doulos*, "slave," in which God manifested himself and gave himself to us.[12] So also do Peter, James, and Jude.[13] Every minister of the gospel, every Christian, is a *doulos*, a "servant" of God, of Jesus Christ and of his brethren.[14] For Jesus' sake, Paul, following his Master, made himself the servant of the faithful and of all men: "For we do not proclaim ourselves; we proclaim Jesus Christ as Lord and ourselves as your slaves for Jesus' sake." (2 Cor 4:5; cf. 1 Cor 9:19). Paul has no intention of "lording over," "domineering" (2 Cor 1:23, the verb *kurieuo*). It is the Lord, not Paul, who enables the faithful to live in the religious relationship of faith. In the same vein, Peter exhorts the elders not to "lord it" over the flock (1 Pet 5:3; verb *katakurieuo*).

This position in relation to Christ and—because of and following Christ—in relation to the faithful, entails for St. Paul a very significant and very conscious manner of behavior. Paul was well able to claim not only his title of apostle, which he always traces back to "God" (see Galatians), but also his apostolic *authority*.[15] Usually, however, he prefers to take his stand—and tells us so—on the spiritual gifts he has received (1 Cor 7:40; 2 Cor 10:7–8; 11:5ff., 23ff.; 12:1–15), on the signs with which God himself is at work, by blessing his servant's labors (2 Cor 3:1–3), on his love and devotion (1 Thess 2:7–12, a passage to be read in its entirety; Phlm 8—9),[16] and finally on his weakness, for God is pleased to act through this too (2 Cor 11:30; 12:5, 9). He refrains from claiming or bringing forward the *rights* that he possesses and is concerned only with the exercise of his duties, in a life entirely devoted to service, preferring to give than to receive.[17] He ceaselessly bases his injunctions not on his own authority, which could enforce them, but on the example and behavior of the Lord, and the whole Christian ethic consists in imitating, or rather continuing, this example.[18] As Paul was the first to set himself this task, so he in turn becomes a model to be followed.[19]

Fundamentally, to have appealed to rights or authority, even though these were received from the Lord, would have brought in an element of *self*. Paul's desire was to be entirely and always in the stream of grace, grace that suffices (2 Cor 12:9), which gives everything unceasingly, in which we find ourselves at ease only when we ourselves *give* without reservation. All of St. Paul's solutions in the realm of what was later called "casuistry" are dictated by these ideas, and in the last resort, by the law of *agape* that rules them, directly from their source in the bosom of the Father, whose own attribute is love (2 Cor 13:13).[20]

The master exacts service. The servant who is a servant "for the sake of Jesus" *gives*, gives even *himself*. This too is the difference between the hireling and the good shepherd (John 10:10ff.). In one way or another, the conduct of the Christian and especially the apostolate—because they lie in the realm of *agape*, of self-giving love, self-sacrificing love—pledge the Christian and especially the apostle to sacrifice, and ultimately to the surrender of life itself. Each time Jesus spoke of his passion, he went on to apply it to the disciples—they must follow their Master even this far.[21] The trials and tribulations of which St. Paul speaks are the sufferings and tribulations of *an apostle*.[22] Peter did not receive the whole world as his flock without hearing that love's utmost was asked of him, without hearing the death he was to die: "Someone else will fasten a belt around you and take you where you do not wish to go" (John 21:15–19).

AUTHORITY AND "MINISTRY"

Our inventory of New Testament texts would be incomplete without a brief look at its vocabulary. Some expressions the New Testament uses frequently; others it avoids or uses only rarely.

Among the latter are those expressing in Greek the ideas of authority and power:

Taxis, "order": ten instances in the New Testament, seven of them in Hebrew in connection with the orders of Aaron and Melchizedech.

Time, in the sense of a dignity or honor, is very rare: used only of Christ, the steward of the house of God (Heb 3:3) and of the priesthood of Aaron and Christ (Heb 5:4).

Arche occurs twelve times in the New Testament in the sense of "power" ("hierarchy" is never used): three times it applies to magistrates, the civil power (Luke 20:20; Titus 3:1): the other nine times to the Powers that Christ has overcome or will overcome. In no case does the word refer to authorities within the Church.

Exousia, "authority, power," is used ninety-three times in the New Testament.[23] Often it refers to the authority of God or Jesus Christ, three times to the authority of earthly magistrates. Seven texts are relevant to our subject, that is, to ecclesiology, the apostolate, the ministry. In five of them, Jesus gives authority to his disciples to cast out devils (Matt 10:1; Mark 3:15; 6:7; Luke 9:1; 10:19). In two, the term refers to the authority vested in an apostle as minister of God's work in the Church (2 Cor 10:8; 13:10).

Epitage, "authority to command, with the power to bind others" (Titus 2:15). When the command comes from God, St. Paul clearly complies with it (Rom 16:26; 1 Cor 7:25; 1 Tim 1:1; Titus 1:3); he possesses this authority and could exercise it (Titus 2:15), but he often prefers not to use it (1 Cor 7:6; 2 Cor 8:8).

I have confined myself here to terms expressing the *idea* of authority. It is certain that authority is included, *as a reality*, in Christ's institution of the apostolate and in the apostles' institution of certain ministries, and similarly in the fact of mission, even when this is not inflated without qualification by the Jewish concept of *saliah*, envoy. We are not at the moment concerned with the reality of authority, which seems to me to be undeniable, but with the notion of it. That is why I have kept to the level of vocabulary.

The term that generally expresses this function in the New Testament is *diakonia*, which means "service," but its specific connotations are so rich and varied that it is best to translate it as "ministry."[24] In the case of particular ministries, all the words designating them refer to a *task* or *activity* as if to a definite service in the community. Frequently, they are borrowings from the vocabulary of everyday life, with no religious connotation; they become religious terms—and then how forcible they are!—only when they are lived with Christ, in Christ, and for Christ. This is true even of the word *ordinari, ordinatio*. Here they are

apostles, doctors, prophets (1 Cor 12:28);

evangelists, teachers (Eph 4:11);

pastors (Eph 4:11; 1 Pet 5:2ff.; John 21:15–17);

bishops, overseers (Acts 20:28; Phil 1:1; 1 Tim 3:2; Titus 1:7);

priests, ancients, elders (Acts 11:30; 14:22; 15:2; 20:17; 21:18; 1 Tim 4:14; 5:17, 19; James 5:14; 1 Pet 5:1);

diaconos, minister (frequently in a general sense of servant; as the title of a function, see Phil 1:1; 1 Tim 3:8ff.);

leader, chief, official in charge (Acts 18:22[?]; Heb 13:7, 17a);

proistamenos, president (Rom 12:8; 1 Thess 5:12; 1 Tim 5:17 [presbyters]);

steward, bailiff, manager ([Luke 12:42]; 1 Cor 4:1; Titus 1:7).

2

HISTORICAL DEVELOPMENT OF AUTHORITY

THE CHURCH OF THE MARTYRS AND MONASTIC CATHOLICISM

The Church of the Martyrs spans the period from the apostles to the peace of Constantine. Here what I call monastic Catholicism spans the period from then to roughly the middle of the eleventh century, with the proviso that the great historical epochs I am distinguishing must not be considered as heterogeneous or as strictly limited to a chronological period before and after which we find none of their features existing. I wondered at first whether it was not necessary, from our present standpoint, to distinguish as two separate periods the Church of the Martyrs and the Church from the fourth to the tenth century. In spite of certain slight reservations, I shall indicate, I do not think this advisable. As regards the idea of authority, they both belong to the same ecclesiological world. Newman calls the five centuries from St. Gregory to St. Anselm the Benedictine period.[1]

The notion of authority in the Church of the Martyrs combines into one of the following three features or values, which we shall deal with one after the other. They are a strong insistence on authority, a very close link with the Christian community, and a marked charismatic or spiritual character.

THE INSISTENCE ON AUTHORITY

The insistence on authority has never been greater than in the writings of St. Ignatius of Antioch (109–10) and of St. Cyprian (245–58). This insistence is all the stronger in that the religious or mystical value of salvation or of grace coincides completely with the juridical status of the authority presiding over a society and regulating its life. This fact is stated repeatedly by Ignatius, Cyprian, and, be it noted, by Irenaeus (circa 180) and St. Hippolytus (circa 200) who, like Origen soon after, calls the bishop "prince." We need only refer to a few of St. Ignatius's formulas. They are so vigorous that critics formerly doubted their authenticity in view of what they considered their outrageous "Catholicism." By being subject to their bishop, the Magnesians or the Trallians are subject to God himself or to Jesus Christ (*Magn.* III, 1–2; cf. VI, 1; *Tral.* II, 1). It is the Spirit who cries out in Ignatius, "Cleave to your bishop, to the presbyterium and the deacons" (*Phil.* VII).

THE LINK WITH THE COMMUNITY

It might almost have been as well to put this characteristic first because, for early Christianity, the primary reality is the *Ecclesia*. This word—and, in this respect, it differs from the word *Church* as very often used today—means the Christian community, the assembly or the unity of Christians. St. Cyprian says, "The Church is the people united to its pontiff, and the flock abiding with its shepherd. This will make you see that the bishop is in the Church and the Church in the bishop."[2] It is this *Ecclesia* in her entirety that exercises her spiritual motherhood by her charity, unity, prayer, and penance; she is the true and adequate reality whose actions are holy and sanctifying.

This same interpretation of *Ecclesia* is found in the liturgical texts, which are the expression of tradition. The *Ecclesia* is the assembly of the brethren established by an act of the Lord and by his presence in their midst. The ancient liturgy has no "I" distinct from the "we" of the whole community. The celebrant, that is, the president of the assembly and the head of the community, speaks in the name of all, for he is one with all its members. Several letters dating from the subapostolic period are written by the community and by its head, and the two are inseparably linked.[3] In these letters, there is a constant alternation of assertions of the hierarchical principle and assertions of the community principle.[4] When in 1950–52, I was preparing my book on the laity, I examined not only the texts but the facts of the early history of the Church. I discovered everywhere in each generation and in the four spheres of faith, worship, the apostolate, and the Church's social life, a union between the hierarchical structure and the communal exercise of all Church activities. The laity took an active part in the life of the Church as a whole. St. Cyprian puts into words a principle echoed on all sides by tradition. He says,

> I have made it a rule, ever since the beginning of my episcopate, to make no decision merely on the strength of my own personal opinion without consulting you [the priests and the deacons], without the approbation of the people.[5]

In fact, the whole Church community, the laity especially, took part in the election of bishops and the choice of ministers. They supplied information for councils and shared in the institution of those customs by which the various communities largely regulated their own lives. Their intervention, as occasion arose, was accepted all the more willingly since the early Church, while possessing a firm canonical structure, wanted to be ready for any movement inspired by the Holy Spirit. And God is pleased to make his will known through the humblest and the least esteemed of his children.

THE MOVEMENT OF THE SPIRIT

Nevertheless, the bishops were the men who possessed the principal *charismatic gifts* in the community. The passage in St. Paul, "Those who are unspiritual do not receive the gifts of God's Spirit, for they are foolishness to them, and they are unable to understand them because they are spiritually discerned. Those who are spiritual discern all things, and they are themselves subject to no one else's scrutiny"

(1 Cor 2:14–15) had all true believers in mind. It was the statement of a principle of Christian anthropology and has been understood as such by tradition. A special application of the text, however, was very soon made concerning the bishops, the heirs of the apostles or of their immediate successors, and like them, being possessed of charismatic gifts as well as preeminent in dignity and authority. In fact, in the early Church, the mystical and the juridical elements were closely interwoven and the idea of grades of spirituality was linked with that of grades of dignity. The bishop was then looked upon as a head or a "prince," and at the same time, as a spiritual man preeminently endowed with the gifts of the Spirit. It was as such that he was chosen, for it was his duty to lead God's people. His actions, and in a more general way, all the decisive factors in the life of the Church, whether due to decisions emanating from the authority of the bishop or of synods, or from some other source, were attributed to God's intervention. A text like the following from the acts of the council held at Carthage in the spring of 252 is evidence of a fact it would be easy to verify in a great number of examples: "It has pleased us, under the inspiration of the Holy Spirit and in accordance with admonitions given by the Lord in many manifest visions."[6] The life of St. Cyprian is marked by visions and supernatural admonitions. From this time forward, we find a continuous series of texts that use, in regard to all the decisive acts in the life of the Church, the words *inspirare*, *inspiratio, revelare, revelatio*, and others of similar type.

In the early Church, authority was that of men who were like princes in a community that was wholly sanctified, *plebs sancta*, and overshadowed by the Spirit of God. The Church leaders were even more conscious of their authority in that they saw it as the vehicle of the mystery of that salvation that God wishes to accomplish in his Church. They wanted to be, and knew that they were, moved by the Spirit, but they also knew that the Spirit inhabits the Christian community, and in the exercise of their authority, they remained closely linked to this community.

FROM CONSTANTINE TO GREGORY VII

One might assume *a priori* that this concept would be more or less perverted or abandoned by the episcopate during the period following the peace of Constantine. The clergy were given important privileges, the bishops became *illustri*, and for all practical purposes, ranked with the senators. They were invested with public authority within the framework of the Empire, even in the sphere of the secular life of the cities. The bishop was the defender of the people, especially of the poor and the weak. He shared in the administration of justice, he exercised a measure of control over the magistrates and the city assemblies. He cooperated in defense preparations (the maintenance of the town walls, for example) and in actual defensive operations. The bishops frequently called on the imperial authority for support. We have only to remember, to take one example, the history of Donatism. Furthermore, Church laws often became laws of the Empire, which undertook to see that they were respected. Under these conditions, we ought perhaps to expect that authority would change its character and that it would acquire a much more secular, much more juridical meaning, based simply on the relation of superior to subordinate. It would cease to open onto the higher sphere of a marked charismatic action on God's part and on to the lowest sphere of the influence of the action of the community, and so close in on itself and become authority for its own sake, authority pure and simple.

Such a danger was very real. It was comparable and in a line with the danger of a Hellenization or rationalization of doctrine resulting from an effort to produce a symbiosis of doctrine and pagan philosophical culture. The two cases are parallel and were more or less contemporary.

Monasticism has often been represented as a protest against a Church that had become too worldly, too rich, too powerful in a physical sense for an eschatological Christianity that taught that the world should be opposed. In monasticism, it was possible for a charismatic or spiritual authority to continue to exist, an authority that should be exercised when the aim is to form the spiritual man, to introduce the soul to "the philosophy of Christ." In fact, this type of authority is found among the patriarchs of monasticism or the legislators of the religious life, the authority of those who are purely and simply "men of God." In the last analysis, this authority is that of the Spirit himself shining through the purity of the *vir Dei*. This type of authority did in fact acquire a kind of autonomy in the Church in relation to the ordinary hierarchical structure. This was the case in the East. Both Origen and the pseudo-Areopagite held views that tended to link the illuminating and sanctifying effect of hierarchical acts with the interior and spiritual holiness of the minister. From the beginning of the eighth century, as a result of the Monothelite quarrel and still more the iconoclast crisis during which the monks had been the champions of orthodoxy, there was a real transfer of spiritual direction and of the exercise of the power of the keys from the hierarchical priesthood to the monks, even when the latter were not priests, because it was clear that they were the genuinely spiritual men and friends of God. As is well known, this Eastern tradition was revived or continued in the institution of the *staretz* or elders of Holy Russia. These monks, who were rarely priests, exercised a wholly spiritual authority as men of God in a ministry of spiritual direction and confession.

Was there not a similar phenomenon in the West, not only in particular cases where a purely spiritual influence was brought to bear, apart from all hierarchical authority (as happens in every period), but in the particular organization of Celtic Christianity down to the twelfth century? There was no diocesan pattern, that is, there were no specific territories under the authority of bishops, but a whole complex of spheres of spiritual influence. A "saint" had his own sphere of influence in which he was in a sense the permanent spiritual lord of a given place. A territory was affiliated to a holy man, and eventually there was a grouping with a monastery at its center, and the jurisdiction belonged to the abbot who was often, but not necessarily, in bishop's orders. Sometimes even, as at Kildare, jurisdiction was in the hands of an abbess. Authority was attributed to the man of God and not to a particular grade in the priestly hierarchy.

Yet it would be a mistake to see any *opposition* between this type of authority and that exercised by the bishops during the period from the peace of Constantine to the Gregorian reform. In the first place, it is a fact that many of these bishops were monks or at least men trained in a monastic setting who ordered their lives on a similar pattern, often with a nostalgic longing for the religious life. To name only a few of these, there are St. Basil, St. John Chrysostom, St. Augustine, St. Martin,

St. Germanus of Auxerre, St. Patrick, Eucherius of Lyons, Faustus of Riez, Lupus of Troyes, Caesarius of Arles, Martin and Fructuosus of Braga, Isidore of Seville, and finally the most representative of them all, St. Gregory the Great. From St. Augustine's time until the twelfth century, all of the archbishops of Canterbury were monks.

The bishop, whether or not he is a monk, is a spiritual man, a man of God. The oldest sections in the Latin ritual of ordination state his duties rather than his powers. The bishop must devote himself to an assiduous study of Holy Scripture, to prayer, fasting, and hospitality. He must welcome, listen to, and help everybody; he must practice almsgiving. He is to edify his people by word of mouth and by the celebration of the liturgy, and in so doing, he is to be aware not of his *dominium* or *potestas*, but of his *ministerium*, to use the words the Catholic West owes to St. Augustine. God is the primal and sovereign agent of this edification. The phrases "God has revealed" and "God has inspired" constantly recur as during the preceding period. Thus a *spiritual* as well as a pastoral authority was exercised by hierarchical authority. This was in accordance with the ideal of *prodesse* as contained in *praeesse*, which had been universally accepted since St. Augustine. Men felt that this was true, even if they were not (yet) Christians. When the praetorian prefect Probus sent his subordinate Ambrose, then only a catechumen, to take up at Milan the post of consul of Liguria and Emilia, he told him, "Go, and act, not as a judge, but as a bishop."[7] A bishop therefore represented a whole ideal of care for men's welfare, of justice, disinterestedness, welcome, in short an essentially moral ideal of authority.

This ideal we find attained by St. Ambrose,[8] St. Augustine, and finally by St. Gregory the Great. The author of the *Regula Pastoralis*, so widely read in the Middle Ages, was in fact himself a living model of the spiritual exercise of authority. Not only did he achieve his ideal of living a life in which personal sanctification and the exercise of the ministry were combined, but he also succeeded in exercising the supreme authority *in a Christian manner*. This means, in the first place, that authority is exercised in a genuine spirit of service and so with a sincere sense of humility. For St. Gregory, the formulas "servant of the servants of God" (*Servus servorum Dei*) and "I am the priests' servant" (*cunctorum sacerdotum servus sum*)[9] were not mere official phrases. Over and above the exercise of authority and in the very act of exercising it, he took a genuine interest in the welfare *of the men* under his command.[10] He loved and respected their progress in virtue as resulting from their own free will. He took care to explain to them the reasons for any of his own decisions in the light of some good or some truth that their souls instinctively sought.[11] In a word, he exercised his authority like a kind of supreme and universal father abbot, combining the tender care of a mother with the authority of a father.[12] For him, the Church was not a vast organization or a system but a community of men moving toward the perfection of charity.

Not all the popes have followed this course. Yet we should note at this point that if Rome succeeded in obtaining, over and above her power, the *authority* of her primacy, it was in large part due to the value and the wisdom of her answers to all the questions that were put to her from every region of Christendom. Genuine authority is moral authority.

Hence, the great bishops of the centuries we have understand-ably called those of monastic Catholicism were very careful to relate authority to its transcendent spiritual principle. They also preserved its relationship to the Christian community, which was still what they understood by the word *ecclesia*. In fact, during this period, the primal and decisive reality in ecclesiology was still the *Ecclesia* itself, that is, the totality, the community, the unity of the faithful. This may appear to be a truism, but ten years of study of and reflection on the history of the ecclesiological doctrines have convinced me that it is not. It is a statement whose importance is primordial. The whole concept of authority in the treatise *De Ecclesia* and the whole balance of the treatise itself depend on it. For the fathers and the early Christians, the *Ecclesia* comes first. Then, in the *Ecclesia*, come the *praepositi ecclesiae*, the presidents or heads of the Christian community.[13]

The head of the Church, the bishop, is in the first place himself a Christian, and he says so. St. Augustine constantly tells his flock, "I am a bishop for your sake, I am a Christian together with you," "a sinner together with you," and "a disciple and a hearer of the Gospel together with you."[14]

The foundation of all this and of patristic ecclesiology, which continued to be that of the early Middle Ages, is doubtless the fact that the Church is composed of men and that all that is done within the Church is aimed formally and immediately at the formation of spiritual men. Ecclesiology and anthropology are not in separate compartments, and the former is a continuation of soteriology, which is itself but one chapter in Christology. This is why all the images and types in Scripture, in which is expressed any aspect of the spiritual destiny of men in relation to the covenant God offers them, are continually and easily applied to the *Ecclesia*. What is involved is not a system or a juridical set-up but a body of men praying, fasting, doing penance, asking for grace, engaging in a spiritual combat, and struggling for the triumph in themselves of the spirit of Jesus Christ. This is why authority is *moral* and requires men who are themselves spiritually alive. On the other hand, it is obvious that if the Church is considered a suprapersonal possessor of rights, a juridical personality enjoying a divine authority conceived as juridical, then these themes from spiritual anthropology no longer apply.

Under such conditions, it is also true that authority is still exercised in conjunction with the community. The celebrated formulas "He who is to preside over all should be chosen by all"[15] and "A bishop should not be imposed on those unwilling to receive him"[16] date from the councils and popes of the fourth and fifth centuries.

One form taken by this effort to win the agreement of the community was the care shown, at least in the fourth and fifth centuries, in reporting to this community or in keeping it informed of facts that today would be carefully withheld from its appraisal or even from its knowledge. We have only to read in this connection the sermons in which Augustine gave his people an account of his conduct and of the principles on which he wished to base the cooperation of his clergy in his work as their bishop.[17] He did not hesitate to go so far as to give a frank statement in public on a delicate business involving one of his priests who had come to an arrangement in which his own private interests had been too cleverly promoted. Who would do anything of the sort today? By giving all his flock an account of the way in which he wanted his priests and clerics to live with him, Augustine lifted the whole life of the *Ecclesia* onto so lucid a plane that he ensured for himself the enlightened and full consent of the faithful.

On the other hand, in the context of the Christian Empire, clerics and bishops obtained important immunities from secular jurisdiction. Later, within the Church herself, canon law was to weave a kind of Noah's cloak around the prestige and honor of clerics, bishops, and Roman dignitaries.[18]

These privileges are part of the body of legal measures that henceforward contributed their share toward making the clergy a class apart. Among these measures, celibacy was one of the most important,[19] but others, such as the introduction of special garb from the end of the early part of the fifth century,[20] effectually initiated a considerable change in the relations between the faithful and the presidents of the community, priests, or bishops. In fact, the difference between the two categories tended to be not only a difference of function as it had been since the beginning within the framework of service in the *Ecclesia*, but a difference in Christian living. Clerics were to observe a special rule of life modeled more or less on that of the monks and inspired by the Levitical regulations of the Old Testament. Thus, whilst in the Church of the Martyrs there was a tension, not inside the Church between the various categories of Christians, but between the *Ecclesia* and the world, henceforth within a society entirely Christian, tension grew inside the Church or within Christian society, between monks or priests on the one hand and laymen on the other. I am well aware that this statement is too simplified and categorical; it needs to be qualified and clarified, and this cannot be done here. It was necessary, however, even at the risk of oversimplification, to draw attention to this point that is extremely important for our subject.

The main lines of the facts we have just summarized remained characteristic of Christianity during the early Middle Ages, as it existed in the West among the nations as they emerged from the barbarian invasion and converted to Catholicism. There were certain differences, however. that I must be allowed to do no more than enumerate here without producing documentary evidence to substantiate their existence: (1) the word *Ecclesia* at this period indicated Christian society and included the Empire or the various kingdoms as well as the Church properly so called; (2) this *Ecclesia* was governed by two authorities, or in the terms used since Gelasius, by two "pre-eminent persons," the royal and the priestly; and (3) the authority of the priest-hood was essentially understood as the authority of the power of the keys, that is, of a sacred power that was both sacramental and judicial, and gave or refused entry into heaven.

Hence, a historical study aiming to cover all the ground would have to consider the concept and exercise of priestly authority in every sphere of social life and over the princes themselves as princes. This is obviously beyond the scope of the present paper.

PRIESTLY AUTHORITY IN THE MIDDLE AGES

We are convinced that the reform begun by St. Leo IX (1049–54) and continued with such vigor by St. Gregory VII (1073–81) represents a decisive turning point from the point of view of ecclesiological doctrines in general and of the notion of authority in particular.

We know that this reform not only aimed, like all reforms, to purify the Church—it was accompanied by powerful spiritual movements in favor of the "apostolic life" such as the canons regular and even the eremitic life—but also to deliver the Church from the power of laymen. It aimed to rid itself of its identification with political society, an identification indicated by the word *Ecclesia* itself, which meant both the mystical Body and the Empire with no distinction made between them. In short, it meant Christian society. To bring this about, Gregory VII claimed for the Church the completely autonomous and sovereign system of rights proper to a spiritual society.

The foundation of the ecclesiastical edifice was the pope whose authority emanated directly from a positive divine institution. Gregory VII claimed the sovereign rights of this authority not only over the Church but also over kings and their kingdoms. To support his claims, he had asked churchmen, beginning with Peter Damian, to discover the maximum number of juridical texts in favor of this view. In fact, a whole series of canonical collections owes its existence to this request. For all of these reasons, the eleventh century reform set in motion a powerful wave of canonical studies. Schools were founded, among them that of Bologna, in which, from this time onward, both the Roman and the canon law were studied together. Research brought to light a great number of texts; efforts were made to classify, harmonize, and systematize these. The science of canon law had well and truly begun.

From the point of view in which we are now interested, there emerged such a considerable development of an authority methodically asserting and claiming its rights, that it is possible to speak of a new chapter in the history of the notion of authority itself, although it is quite true that the situation was not entirely new and that popes or bishops had already asserted and claimed such rights. This development was so powerful because it was not purely juridical or purely academic. On the contrary, it was due to powerful personalities and a vast and profound "mystique." First, St. Gregory VII, then St. Anselm of Canterbury, and later St. Thomas Becket, who became immensely popular after his death: these are the men who initiated or brought forward these assertions or this claim to these rights. Not that they claimed them for themselves personally (they were wholly disinterested), but for their authority, and based on a very theological and very supernatural "mystique." What interested them all was absolute *Justice*, that is, a theonomy (a divine law) that was expressed in a system of Church law, and even more precisely in the rights of the pontiff. The same attitude is found in Innocent III, though perhaps not in Innocent IV who was more strictly a jurist, but certainly in Boniface VIII in his own somewhat questionable and equivocal way. The strength of a movement always lies in its "mystique." In the movement we are now considering, what was characteristic was the fact that its "mystique" was formulated in and, one might almost say, invested with legal principles, and a genuine political theology.

This was not achieved without submitting certain themes and certain texts to a legalistic interpretation. I myself attach very great importance to one fact that I have personally studied in a few given cases, namely, the translation into terms of law (and of rights!) together with a specific application to the pope and to the pope alone, of themes and texts that originally and, up to this period, belonged to the realm of spiritual anthropology. I have studied this change of level and meaning in the case of Jeremiah 1:10 ("See, today I appoint you over nations and over kingdoms, / to pluck up and to pull down, / to destroy and to overthrow, / to build and to plant"), in the case of 1 Corinthians 2:15 and 6:3 ("Those who are spiritual discern all things, and they are themselves subject to no one else's scrutiny....Do you not know that we are to judge angels—to say nothing of ordinary matters?"), less directly and less fully in the case of 1 Peter 2:9 ("You are...a royal priesthood"), and in a few other instances. Jeremiah 1:10 becomes an assertion of the supreme authority of the pope and of his right to depose kings. One of the last occasions in which this text was used in this sense was in Pius V's bull *Regnans in excelsis* deposing Queen Elizabeth I (Elizabeth II harbored no resentment; she visited Pius V's successor, John XXIII, on the very day allotted in the calendar to the feast of the former.) 1 Corinthians 15 becomes a new formulation of the old principle *Prima Sedes a nemine judicatur* and 1 Corinthians 6:3, *angelos judicabimus, quanto magis saecularia* becomes an assertion of the right of priests, but more especially and supremely of the right of the pope, to judge secular powers.

We have also studied a fact that seems to have escaped Msgr. Michel Maccarone, who has written the history of the expression *Vicarius Christi* as a papal title. The use of the title has continued but its meaning has changed. Its older sense in Catholic *theology* was that of a visible representation of a transcendent or heavenly power *that was actually active* in its earthly representative. The context and atmosphere surrounding this idea were those of the actuality of the action of God, Christ, and the saints working in their representative. This is a very sacramental, iconological concept, linked to the idea of constant "presences" of God and the celestial powers in our earthly sphere. It is this quality of actuality and of a "vertical" descent and a presence that has its source in the celebrated text in Luke 10:16, "Whoever listens to you listens to me, and whoever rejects you rejects me." Although this quality does not disappear, it is overlaid by another quality that also is not entirely new. What is new is its marked predominance over the former one, namely, the idea of a "power" given at the beginning by someone, by Christ, to his "vicar," that is, to a representative who takes his place and who hands on to those who come after him, in a historical sequence of transmission and succession, the power thus received. The predominant feature is not a vertical movement, an actual presence, an iconological representation, but the "horizontal" transmission of a power vested in the earthly jurisdiction and that, although received from on high, is yet genuinely possessed by this jurisdiction, which uses it in the same way as any authority may use the power attached to it.

The modern "mystique" of authority in the Church is derived from the movement whose characteristics we just described. But— and this is where its strength lies, once again, strength comes from the "mystique" and not from the legal aspect—it has combined the actuality of the power possessed with the vision of the "vertical" descent of divine power upon the actual historic authority. One is actually obeying God when one obeys his representative. Unless I am mistaken, this is, in particular, the view of St. Ignatius Loyola as it is explained, for example, by Fr. Hugo Rahner.[21] Fr. Rahner moreover does not find any difficulty in linking St. Ignatius Loyola with the first Ignatius of Antioch, with St. Irenaeus and St. Augustine (who inspired Gregory VII), and so on. This shows that although there was an innovation, it was still in continuity with a tradition. However, I believe that the spirit of the time introduced something new into this continuity, namely, a certain legalistic aspect.

THE CHURCH IS...

We see this legalism at work in the importance attached to the formal validity of authority, to its possession of a title in law. There is no insistence on the need of an actual intervention of God's grace, nor therefore on the need for man to pray for this intervention and to prepare for it by bodily mortification, by explicitly relating the exercise of authority to sacred acts such as the celebration of the mysteries, fasting, chastity, prayer, and the like. In short, legalism is characteristic of an ecclesiology unrelated to spiritual anthropology, and for which the word *Ecclesia* indicates not so much the body of the faithful as the system, the apparatus, the impersonal depositary of the system of rights whose representatives are the clergy or, as it is now called, the hierarchy, and ultimately the pope and the Roman Curia.

It is a fact that *Church* is sometimes understood by the theorists of ecclesiastical power or papal authority as indicating clerics, priests, and the pope. This use of the word was completely unknown to the fathers and the liturgy. It is a fact that in a large number of modern documents, the word *church* indicates the priestly government or even quite simply this government's Roman courts. It is distinct from the faithful, from men in general, and outside and above them. Here is one example from hundreds that could be given: "The Church is given the task of feeding the flock of Jesus Christ."[22] But the Church is herself this flock. This change of meaning is serious. In the first place, it is out of keeping with scriptural, patristic, and liturgical usage. Furthermore, it runs the risk of separating the "Church" from the sphere in which men are trained in the spiritual life. I would like to point out in this respect a problem that, as far as I know, has never been considered, namely, the application of the directives of the gospel, not only to individuals but to the Church as such. Is it the individual alone who must be the servant and not the master, who must forgive offences, bless his enemies and not curse them? Have themes such as these any longer a place in an ecclesiology identified in practice with a treatise on public ecclesiastical law?

Furthermore, under these conditions, instead of being seen as a relationship of superior to subordinate *within* the vast system of mutual love and service between Christians who are Christians as the result of a grace for which each is accountable to all, does not authority run the risk of being posited *first and foremost as authority for its own sake*, and so of being looked upon in a purely juridical and sociological way, and not from a spiritual and Christian standpoint?

It is obvious that Christians and men of God anxious to work for his kingdom and devoid of all self-interest have shaped their lives in accordance with this juridical concept. At a more prosaic level, this is true of conscientious churchmen, but it has favored the growth of the idea of the priest as *governing* his parish, as exercising a *regime*, as *ruler*. It has favored the growth of the idea of the bishop and the pope as *judges*, of the pope as a *sovereign*, since he is the vicar of Christ, *Rex regum et Dominus dominantium* (King of kings and Lord of lords).[23] It has favored the growth of the idea of the Church as *queen* of mankind, since she is the Bride of Christ who is the ruler of the world.[24] It cannot be denied that, from the eleventh century onward, authority and in particular the supreme authority of the pope, borrowed many of the features of the vocabulary, insignia, ceremonial style, and ideology of the imperial court. These factors sometimes go back to pagan days and even, by way of the Hellenistic monarchy of Alexander, to the Persian paganism of the fourth century BC. Even the title of *Curia* assumed by the papal administration was borrowed from the secular vocabulary and, at the time, there were those who did not fail to point this out.[25]

CRITICAL REACTIONS

Protests were made. We shall not cease to insist that one of these has never been taken seriously enough, either at the time or since, by the historiographers. I refer to the protest represented by the more or less antiecclesiastical spiritual movements so frequent in the twelfth century and which continued in the Franciscan spiritual movement down to the fourteenth century when it was succeeded by Lollardism and subsequently by the Hussite movement. All of these movements, each from its own point of view and within its own terms of reference, said the same thing: "Less pomp and more of the Gospel! You are Constantine's Church, not the Church of the apostles." St. Bernard, who did battle with Arnold of Brescia, Henri de Lausanne, and the neo-Manicheans, did not scruple to repeat these explosive criticisms. He wrote to Eugenius III:

> You allow yourself to be over-burdened with decisions you have to give in all kinds of external and secular cases. As far as you are concerned, I hear of nothing but awards and "laws." All this, as well as claims to prestige and riches, goes back to Constantine not to Peter.[26]

In a more general and perhaps more profound way, theology preserved many elements of the ancient ecclesiology in a balanced view that lasted until the death of the two greatest thirteenth-century doctors, Thomas and Bonaventure. In St. Thomas, for example, the idea of the Church as *congregatio fidelium* (gathering of the faithful) is very much alive, and includes the theology of the return to God of humankind made in his image. Authority is not looked upon as a mere formal and juridical value; it is linked to the spiritual gifts, to the achievement of Christian perfection, which is the perfection of charity, and so, by the same token, to the achievement of spiritual liberty and the gift of self in loving service. Matthew 16:19 is interpreted as referring principally to Peter's confession of faith. The theology of the new law, as formulated in the Ia, IIae q. 106, and in the scriptural commentaries, is completely evangelical and certainly represents a fundamental category in St. Thomas's ecclesiology.

We should be guilty of a serious omission if we also failed to mention what we might call the right of conscience. This principle was a vital force down to the Reformation, after which the condemnation of its abuse involved the end of its use. This is a vast field of research demanding special study. It includes, to begin with, the right of resistance to tyranny in the political sphere, and the right to enter religion or to change from one order to another. It then deals with the protection of the poor and the weak— a traditional function of episcopal authority—and the notions of unjust excommunication, the right of protest, the right also to disobey *filialiter et obedienter* (in a spirit of filial obedience), to quote from a letter of Robert Grosseteste to the pope.[27]

Harnack remarked that it was at the time when the formulation of the nature of ecclesiastical power had reached its point of perfection that this power began to be questioned, denied, and attacked. It is a fact that the authority of prelates of every degree was never insisted on so much as in the fourteenth and fifteenth centuries. The thunderclap of October 31, 1517, was only the first of a violent storm. On the European continent, the Reformation refused the right of any human authority whatsoever to enter into the field of man's religious relationship with God. This relationship was to be conditioned by the authority of God alone, and this authority was simply and solely that of his word as contained in Scripture.

FROM THE COUNCIL OF TRENT UNTIL TODAY

The Reformation questioned authority, not only in its historical forms, but as a principle. And the Reformation was roughly contemporary with the rise of the great forces that created the modern world (the sciences of observation, the primacy of individual personality, the passion for invention and continual progress, historical and philosophical criticism, perhaps even the beginnings of rationalism).

The Church's reaction became clear from the time of the Council of Trent onward. It consisted in the twofold process that the Church normally brings into operation when she is seriously challenged. On the one hand, she reasserted her authority and gave it a greater degree of centralization. On the other hand, she revised the idea and the practice of authority on the moral and pastoral planes.

AUTHORITY CHALLENGED AND ASSERTED

She reasserted her authority and not only her own, but the authority of God, of his revelation (Vatican I), of Christ (Christ the King), of the state (encyclicals of Leo XIII), and the authority of parents. Ecclesiology, as far as the instruction of clerics and of the faithful is concerned, became fixed in a set pattern in which the question of authority is so predominant that the whole treatise is more like a hierarchiology or a treatise on public law. In this assertion of authority, the papacy receives the lion's share. The idea of authority, the exercise of authority in contemporary Catholicism, are first and foremost the idea and the exercise of papal authority. The pope is really *episcopus universalis*. Each individual Catholic has a much more immediate relationship with him than with his own bishop, as far as the general pattern of his Christian life is concerned. The encyclicals tell him what he ought to think, the liturgy is regulated by Roman documents, as are also fasting, canonical preparation for marriage, the *ratio studiorum* of seminaries, and canonically erected faculties. The saints we venerate are those canonized by Rome; religious congregations ask Rome for the authorization of their rule and it is from Rome that the secular Institutes have received theirs. Rome intervenes directly in the question of adapting apostolic methods to the needs of the times (for example, worker priests, *Mission de France*). She keeps a sharp eye on publications, books, reviews, catechisms, and occasionally orders their suppression. In short, the exercise of authority in the modern Catholic Church is largely that of its central and supreme seat in Rome.

At a time when the modern world is attempting to build its life on the principle of the individual personality, even to the point of disregarding or denying the objective rights of God and of his law, the Catholic Church since the sixteenth century has put into practice a genuine "mystique" of authority in which the influence of the Society of Jesus has doubtless played its part. This "mystique" may be characterized as the notion of a complete identification of God's will with the institutional form of authority. In the latter, it is God himself whose voice we hear and heed. The fairly wide margin that the Middle Ages still left for the subordinate's opinion is, for all practical purposes, reduced almost to nothing. The pope is the visible Christ, "gentle Christ on earth," as St. Catherine had already said, and every superior is to some extent the visible Christ. Some have even spoken of a real presence of Christ under the pontifical species. Furthermore, the present period has seen, in France at least, a frequent and new use of the terms *hierarchy* and *magisterium*,[28] which, at the level of terminology, indicate a healthy but very powerful insistence on authority.

A certain absolutist sense given to authority and to obedience[29] presupposes a whole development in ecclesiological ideas. To give an account of this growth would involve nothing less than a complete history of the ideas in question. I must be content to stress one point that seems to me to be of more than marginal importance. The image of the Bride of Christ, as applied to the Church, was drawn at a very early date toward the image of the Body by the Pauline theme of the "one body" (see Eph 5:22–33). From both the biblical and the theological aspects, these images are complementary yet distinct. *Body* indicates identity, *bride* indicates otherness, a face-to-face encounter, the Church related to Christ as to her Lord, her head in the sense of Lord. To the extent that the theme of the Church as bride has been absorbed into that of the Church as the Body of Christ, the authority of God has been seen as wholly, one might almost say physically and automatically, present in the authority of the Church. The absolute standard of the divine authority has become, so it would seem, identified with and invested in the human standard of the ecclesiastical authorities. It is true that during the eleventh- and twelfth-century struggles between the priesthood and the secular powers, arguments were based on the rights of the Church as the Bride of Christ and so the Mother of Christians, and these rights were those of God himself. It is obvious that this development would scarcely have been possible if there had been no progress beyond the ancient meaning of *Ecclesia* as indicating the Christian community.

PASTORAL RESPONSIBILITIES

If the medieval clergy, who did not have to go out in search of their flock and who enjoyed considerable privileges, were scarcely called on to show zeal, the clergy of today are. The Council of Trent, by the impetus it provided and the measures it took, began the creation of a new clergy.[30] Previously, the priesthood often existed apart from personal holiness of life, in spite of the fact that councils and episcopal regulations never ceased to insist on the need for priests to be holy men. After the Council of Trent, especially in France during the seventeenth century, priests were given rules of conduct similar to those of the religious life: mortification, prayer, avoidance of every kind of worldliness, etcetera. At the same time, the clergy emerged from the uncultured state so often characteristic of its members in the Middle Ages. A link was reforged, somewhat like that which existed in the patristic period, between the office or the authority and the personal religious quality of the priest's life.

Yet there is one important difference between the nineteenth century or even the first years of the twentieth, and the fourth or fifth centuries: the priesthood is much less monastic, if not from the ascetical point of view, at least from that of the life of contemplation, of the assiduous study of Scripture, of preaching based on the bible and the mysteries of the faith. The bishops have always been absorbed by the cares of administration, or by matters in dispute. This is true of the bishops in the fourth, fifth, and sixth centuries and still more of those of the twelfth to the fifteenth, and these were involved in more secular business.[31] In our own times, they are absorbed by administrative and financial worries. Fr. Combalot humorously observed in the middle of the nineteenth century, "Instead of saying, 'Receive the pastoral staff,' it would be more to the point to say 'Receive the pen of administration, so you can write, write, write, for all eternity'!"[32] As for priests, their time is ceaselessly taken up with pastoral "cases," with a ministry of personal help and support, with repair and rescue work. But all of them, bishops and priests, have a very keen sense of their pastoral and apostolic responsibility. The adjective *apostolic* represents in itself a whole program, it signifies a historical change in the application of the term *apostolic*, which in modern times, has come to mean "zealous" and "having the missionary spirit." It cannot be denied that the exercise of authority in the Church today is marked by a predominance of pastoral care over rank, of tasks and responsibilities over the claiming of privileges. Yet an ecclesiology that is still too juridical, too remote from spiritual anthropology, continues to give a somewhat external character to the aims of authority, a character that is sometimes inclined to be sociological rather than interior and spiritual. "The Church is anxious to do a great deal of governing, but she gives very little education."[33] However, a post-Constantinian situation increasingly makes it imperative that, in a world where institutions are no longer enough for the believers' needs, priests should concentrate on training and sustaining men who possess strong personal convictions. Hence, the mid-twentieth century is characterized by the rediscovery of men who are truly Christian *in their humanity itself*. There can be no doubt that authority will have increasingly to recover the spiritual character of the Church of the Martyrs and the fathers and to take as its aim the building up of communities of Christian men.

In the nineteenth century, romantic literature and often also history had spread the idea that power and the holding of very high office offered an opportunity for greater enjoyment, for complete freedom to do as one liked, and for advancing oneself. The popes of the nineteenth and the twentieth centuries and with them the whole body of the bishops have stood before the eyes of the whole world as men for whom power is responsibility and authority service.

If the history we have outlined had to be summarized in a few significant phrases and a few representative figures, we should doubtless say that for the Church of the Martyrs, the key words are *Lord* and *diaconia*, its typical hero: St. Paul. For the Church of the fathers and the monk-bishops, the words are *Ecclesia, praepositi ecclesiae, Deus inspiravit, ministerium*; the typical heroes: Ignatius of Antioch and Cyprian, Ambrose, Chrysostom, Augustine, Gregory the Great. For the medieval period, the words are *Vicarius Christi, caput, Sponsa-Mater-Magistra, regere, potestas*, and the typical heroes: St. Gregory VII and St. Thomas Becket. For the modern or post-Tridentine period, the words are *the Church* when its leaders are really meant, or *the Hierarchy, the Magisterium*, but also *the laity* and *apostolic*; and the typical heroes are St. Ignatius Loyola, St. Charles Borromeo, the *Pius-Päpste*, that is, Pius IX to Pius XII, Cardinal Suhard.

An overall view of this development reveals its obvious direction, namely, toward a development of ecclesiology itself. One's first examination of any phenomenon is always all embracing. It may be less exact than subsequent analyses but it includes far more. The community, the *Ecclesia*, was first examined, then increasing attention was paid to the *potestas* of its head.[34] The first thing to be seen was the community *composed of Christian men*; then its structural pattern, its organization was examined. Everything was initially attributed to the transcendent cause, then the part played by ecclesiastics as "means" became more clear, and not only so, but the consideration of their function absorbed attention almost to the exclusion of everything else, it being understood once and for all that God is the origin of all. The status of ecclesiastical authority is examined in detail. The history of the exegesis of Matthew 16:18–19 is very instructive in this respect. Formerly, "this rock" was taken to mean the "stone" of the confession of faith, and insistence was laid on Christ as the foundation. Later, the text was held to refer to Peter alone. Similarly, the Virgin Mary was first seen as the mother of Christ, who is God, later her own privileges were studied in detail. In ecclesiology, God initially was considered above all as directly at work; subsequently, attention turned to the created institution that vicariously possesses the powers given by God and of which it is the depositary.

Now we live in the period of rediscovery in breadth and depth of our own heritage. This is due above all to the active investigation of the permanent sources: Scripture, tradition, the fathers, the liturgy. This return to the sources has already begun to emphasize the necessity of a certain rediscovery of the two religious realities by reference to which authority must find out the truth about itself. They are the living God active among us through his grace, and the holy community and brotherhood of the faithful. It is by setting authority in an authentic relationship with these two Christian realities that we shall be able to go beyond legalism that consists in seeing the formal validity of phenomena without penetrating to their meaning. The movement back to the sources must go forward until it restores a completely evangelical concept of authority, a concept that will be both fully supernatural and fully communal. We are on the right road, we have gone far to recover the *agape* beyond mere moralism, the function of the laity, the community, and our mission and service, as dimensions essential to and coextensive with Christian life. We have a better understanding of the religious implications of the covenant, and these involve our acceptance of God's gift through faith, and the life of this gift of God within us through the *agape*, the *diaconia*, witness, and thanksgiving. And this is all of a piece and stands or falls as such. Since we are returning to a pre-Constantinian situation in a pagan world, since we are aware that we are in a minority and that it is our task to preach Jesus Christ, we are doubtless approaching a period in which, while we shall lose nothing of value acquired in the course of history, we shall recover wholly evangelical ways of exercising authority in the new world in which God calls us to serve him.

3

THE CHRISTIAN CONCEPT OF AUTHORITY

The pronouncements of Jesus and the apostles on the subject, and the passages from New Testament literature that I have quoted, lead us to reflect on the actual concept of authority in the New Testament. It would not be enough simply to conclude that authority must be exercised in a spirit of personal unselfishness and service, though of course this would lead to genuine and profitable developments. It is true that the good shepherd gives his life for his sheep, does not feed himself but seeks the good of his flock.[1] It is true that he must not be demanding or grasping, but must make every effort not to be a burden to any in his care.[2] It is true that the faithful are our masters, since we are their servants: their welfare must decide how our effort shall be applied.[3] To know all this not by the intellect alone but in heart and conscience has been and never ceases to be the principle of true evangelical holiness for those who have offices of command in the Church and in the world. The measure of all things, in Christianity, is indeed the spirit of the beatitudes. This is an admitted fact: authority, in the Church, is "not domination, does not impose itself by force; it is service, humility, unselfishness, self-sacrifice."[4]

THE CHURCH ITINERANT

Jesus, however, was not content simply to remind men of the spirit in which authority must be exercised, or to transfer authority from the scribes and rabbis to the apostles, from the priesthood of Aaron to the ministers of the gospel. He radically transformed the whole character and even the nature of authority. And in the same way, he was not content simply to replace the sacrifice of Moses and the priesthood of Aaron by another sacrifice and another priesthood, still of the same nature: he transposed them to another plane of reality. This is more than an analogy with the case of men. Sacrifice and priesthood, and also law, "sabbath," covenant and temple, are bound up together so closely that one cannot change without the other changing, and the same "newness" affects them all when the Son of God became flesh and the Holy Spirit was given (see Heb and 2 Cor 3).

The newness lies in this: we have passed from signs, announcements, or preparations to realities. Rather, we have taken a decisive step toward this passing over to reality. For *pure* reality is eschatological: it corresponds with the state in which all dominion and power shall be brought into subjection, when the externals that afflict us shall be things of the past, when perfect interiority shall be established, rooted in the final condition, "God all in all."[5]

Midway between the synagogue and the kingdom whose embryo she is in this world, the Church is the place where sacrifice, priesthood, law, Sabbath, and covenant are made new, as befits the time (*eon*) of Christ's coming and the gift of the Spirit. From then on, they are in the hearts of men. Sacrifice and priesthood are spiritual, which does not mean metaphorical but corresponding to God's working *in man*. The temple, the place of the presence of God, is the community of the faithful, a spiritual house of living stones, wherein are offered spiritual sacrifices acceptable to God through Jesus Christ (1 Pet 2:5; cf. 1 Cor 3:10–17; Eph 2:19–22; 4:11–16, etc.). There are still *things* in the Church exterior to man and God, because she is not yet pure reality: there are still sacraments, churches built of stone, ceremonies, powers, a coercive form of law, and so on. But all that is secondary and subordinate to the essential, which is men and the grace of the Holy

Spirit within them.[6] The decisive value of what exists in the Church lies not in *things* as things but in living men who, through Christ and in view of his plenitude, build up the Body of Christ or the Temple of God, by faith and charity. Everything is relative to the living Body of Christ, which is made up of the faithful. "You are the body of Christ and individually members of it."[7] That is the fundamental fact underlying our whole theme. In New Testament and patristic texts, the Church is never separated from the Christian life of Christian men, as a *thing* would be; the very word *Ecclesia* approximates very closely in meaning to what we now call the Christian community.

GOD ALL IN ALL

There is one single source for the building up of this Christian community, Jesus Christ, the Head from which the Body has its whole life and increase (Eph 4:15ff.; Col 2:18ff.), the foundation-stone on which—it can almost be said, in which—the whole temple is built (Eph 2:19–22; 1 Pet 2:4ff.). But from Christ onward, all that each receives is directed to the building up of his Body. So each becomes a means of life and growth for all the rest.

Due allowance made, the same holds good of the physical universe because this too, in its own way, forms a whole. With certain necessary transpositions, it is true of the spiritual sphere of destinies that are personal and yet entirely of Christ. That is why St. Peter gives this general rule, of prime importance for us all: "Like good stewards of the manifold grace of God, serve one another with whatever gift each of you has received."[8] And that too is why St. Paul repeats that, in the Body of Christ, each is the servant of all.[9]

In this statute of the life of the Body we can see an anticipation, a sign, a far-off hint of "God all in all." In fact, no Christian attitude can be considered in only two terms. Many pronouncements of Christian attitudes or, if one prefers it, of Christian ethics, are paralleled by very similar pronouncements from such schools of philosophy as Stoicism. But closer inspection reveals a very important difference: pronouncements on Christian ethics or Christian attitudes are not located only on the plane of a human perfection to be striven after, they always flow from their source, as it were, or proceed from their foundation—the attitude and, in the end, the nature of God, revealed to us in human terms in Jesus Christ. Of everything a Christian receives, everything by which he lives and for which he is accountable to his fellows, God is the only source. Because this is so, because he himself does give to all, we too owe to all what we receive from him.

> Now there are varieties of gifts, but the same Spirit; and there are varieties of services, but the same Lord; and there are varieties of activities, but it is the same God who activates all of them in everyone….All these are activated by one and the same Spirit, who allots to each one individually just as the Spirit chooses. (1 Cor 12:4–6, 11; for context, see Eph 4:4–16)

After St. Paul, hear what Bernanos, a Christian says:

> Life teaches me that no man is consoled in this world who has not first given consolation, that we receive nothing that we have not first given. Between us there is only exchange. God alone gives, only God.[10]

JESUS CHRIST, THE ONLY LORD

We are now in a better position to understand the Christian idea of hierarchical office as service. It comes within the compass of the great truths we have just recalled: there is only one Lord; he distributes his gifts to individuals for the service of all and the building up of the Body-Temple; so each one of us, as the disciple of Jesus Christ, becomes the debtor or servant of all. Hierarchical offices organize this service. Fr. L. Laberthonnière has very rightly said (though he was mistaken in thinking that he was in contradiction with St. Thomas, when he was in fact doing little but repeat him):

The exercise of authority in general is only one of the forms of what we each have to do through others and for others to further our common destiny.[11]

St. Paul expressly says that ordained ministers organize the ministry of the saints, that is, of Christians (Eph 4:12). They organize it, but they also invigorate and animate it and drive it forward. They are the drivers and the governors of the Body in that condition of responsibility and universal service that is the Christian condition itself.

To this end, there are temporary orders that relate to individuals, the gifts they have received, the inner call they have answered, the circumstances in which life and providence have placed them. We sometimes speak of charisms in this sense, and this is allowable, if we are careful to remember that *charism* means simply "spiritual gifts," and that established ministries by no means stand outside the charismatic order. There are also permanent orders, which organize the Christian ministry in the sense of *diakonia*, that is, the whole Church seen as service, exercising the ministry, which might equally well be called the service, of the word or of worship.[12] Although it is often impossible to fix the frontier between the two domains, the subject of charisms, more particularly in teaching, is sometimes a regular ministry, sometimes the faithful independently of any previous nomination or ordination.[13]

The subsequent life of the Church developed along lines dictated by a separation, perhaps too clear-cut, between the two orders—which could be described as *ex spiritu* (by virtue of spiritual gifts) and *ex officio* (by virtue of an office), gifts of the individual and gifts of function. To keep them apart, and above all, to regard the order of function as something alien to the order of personal spiritual gifts, would be a betrayal of the New Testament, and of theological tradition too. St. Gregory links the vocation of ministers with the spiritual gifts they have received, which they would forfeit if they refused the charge of the episcopate, having received them to use for the good of others, in imitation of Christ. St. Thomas never separates the spiritual gifts of the individual from function, and what he wrote about the apostles and the episcopate is significant in this connection.

However, let us note here a general scheme that we shall do well to keep in mind, for it throws light on many ecclesiological or pastoral problems. *Mission*, in its widest sense, is a *task* entrusted by the sender to his envoy, with resources sufficient for its accomplishment. These resources may either be simply and generally the spiritual gifts of Christian life, or particular gifts corresponding to election and vocation to the apostolate in its strict sense. In the first case, the mission is simply the moral responsibility to serve, which is represented by Christian life as such or included in every grace from God; in the second case, the mission is election, call and mandate properly speaking, with the gifts of authority and power assignable to them, without prejudice to the spiritual gifts that accompany the formal mandate of the apostolate.

All the moral-ascetic values, with which some authors tend to identify the New Testament's remarks on the hierarchy as service, are equally to be found in an explanation of these passages, which reaches to the very nature of Christian hierarchy: disinterestedness, seeking not one's own good but the good of others, seeking not one's own glory but the master's, and so on.[14] Indeed, it is here that these values find their deepest expression.

HUMAN RELATIONSHIPS "IN THE LORD"

Everything springs from the fact that in Christianity, relationships between people, or between the faithful and things, that is, the relationships that weave the fabric of our life on the horizontal plane of this world, are repeated or assumed into the vertical relationship of love that runs from God to us, and the vertical relationship of faith that runs from us to him. We see this in St. Paul, in his three types of relationships: with the outsider or the foreigner (Jew and Greek, or Greek and barbarian); between employer and employed, master and subordinate (slave/freeman); between man and woman (see Gal 3:28; Col 3:11; Phlm). The relation between slave and freeman, even between woman and man, is subordination. But if this human relationship is lived "in the Lord," and so stems from him and is lived according to him, it ceases to be the natural relationship recognized by the civil code, sociology, economics, or politics. It changes direction radically.

It is no longer a relationship in two terms on the horizontal plane, one term opposed to the other, but in three terms, situated vertically. Will, providence, and the gift of God travel through me as it were from top to bottom, and are relayed through me, without removing from me the sublime duty of willing acceptance. Everyone, according to his place in the earthly organism, whether of society or the Church (which, in this world, is a society and not a pure communion of spiritual inwardness), bears the duty of care (*cura*) that God himself and his Christ have for their own, and in some measure entrust to us: "Feed *my* sheep."[15]

This duty is laid on every Christian, in a general way, with Christianity itself. Some receive it a second time, and in new fashion, when they are ordained to a position of authority. Authority is indeed a title in its own right, but the title is conferred within a general order of service and, in Christianity, has no existence outside this order. It is no longer defined as one man's ownership of or right over other men but first and fundamentally as a duty laid on us by God, as a responsibility and obligation entrusted to us:

> If I proclaim the gospel, this gives me no ground for boasting, for an obligation is laid on me....For if I do this of my own will, I have a reward; but if not of my own will, I am entrusted with a commission. What then is my reward? Just this: that in my proclamation I may make the gospel free of charge, so as not to make full use of my rights in the gospel. (1 Cor 9:16–18)

In the gospel, the dignity of the apostolate is linked with the person of Jesus and a mission received from him; this is a clear indication that the dignity is given as a duty and obligation, not formally nor primarily as a right that belongs to the apostle. Authority in the gospel is a relationship of *sub et supra* (subordination and authority) within the general relationship of service, which is the necessary accompaniment of being a Christian. It is a duty, not a right:[16] "*nec imperio praesidere, sed ministerio*: to exercise authority not as a power, but as a service."[17] As St. Bernard says, it is *cura* (what one has responsibility for, but does not own), not *dominium* (what one is master of).[18]

VOCATION TO SERVICE

St. Thomas saw the episcopate as consecration to a life lived in the charity of Christ, in total and definitive self-giving for the salvation of men.[19] Poverty and obedience are the ascetic discipline of the religious; the bishop's asceticism is self-dedication to all the battles and sacrifices of the apostolate, even to the point of giving his life, if need be.[20] This view of the episcopate is classic in the Church, and its theme has been taken up and developed in many treatises, especially since the Council of Trent.[21] It expresses the Catholic ideal of the bishop. It is important that we should see in it not only the *ideal*, but the *idea*, of the episcopate, pursuing this line of thought until we arrive at the *notion* of the hierarchy as service. This will lead us, if not to revise, at least to define our ideas on the role of the priesthood and the meaning of ordination, even on the vocation to the priesthood, the first step on the road that leads through seminary or training college to ordination. Before he becomes a priest, that is, before he is ordained to a directing post in the great Christian function of service, a minister of the Church is a Christian. *"Vobis sum episcopus, vobiscum christianus*: I am a bishop for your sake but I am a Christian together with you."

The whole Body is dedicated to the ministry and to witness. Moreover, the whole Body is consecrated, the whole Body is priestly: 1 Peter 2:4ff.; Exodus 19:6. But the Body is organized according to the will of God, who is the God not of dissension but of peace (1 Cor 14:33; cf. 40). God calls some of his servants to become leaders in service and to this leadership there are two titles, both of which we must clearly understand: (1) the title of one who knits together and organizes the service of all, making it truly a service of the whole Body, a communal ministry; and (2) the title of a minister of the sacraments, of the gifts Christ makes to his people within the framework of the structures of the covenant, which cannot be reduced to the gifts he makes to men directly and personally. These two titles correspond to the two senses in which the priest is mediator: as an intermediary (the second title), and as the central point in whom and because of whom the charity of the faithful is knit together.

What we have said about the priest may equally be applied to the bishop, to the diocese, or to the universal Church.

In this perspective, ordination is not only the hierarchical transmission of powers but also the consecration of the action by which the Church orders her charity and builds herself into a body in realization of the ministry that is concomitant with the state of being a Christian. To have a vocation to the priesthood, to prepare and present oneself for ordination, and eventually to receive consecration from the bishop is to be called to Christian service in a more concentrated, more specific way, to be qualified to become a leader in this service and publicly to accept its character, having first accepted it in one's heart and striven to be worthy of it. It follows that the Church, that is, the fellowship of all Christians, should play a large part in awakening the sense of vocation in training ministers, and finally in their ordination. If we do not give all this, and the priesthood itself, its rightful place within the framework of the community of the faithful, we turn our backs on the meaning that the New Testament gives these realities.

So the whole Church bears the priesthood of those who, within her, are called to the ministry. She is wholly responsible for the idea that her hierarchical ministers have of the nature of their authority, and for the way in which they exercise it. If they are treated as potentates, they will become potentates. If they are deferred to with servility, it will be too easy for them to let their lives be ruined by the spirit of domination, which is very tenacious of life in the heathen that still survives in each one of us.

AUTHORITY IN CHARITY

Perhaps my account, however accurate in dealing with the New Testament texts, has left a certain uneasiness in the minds of some of my readers. Surely it has called into question the reality of the functions of the ministry as *hierarchical powers*. What is this authority whose very *nature* is service? Should we not revert to the conception that has been so summarily criticized: conceive the *nature* of authority as in the line of juridical power, *secundum sub et supra*, and keep the "mystique" of service for the moral order of its *use*: in short, make it a question of personal virtue?

An authority most certainly does exist in the Church. The New Testament not only supposes or expressly affirms the existence of offices of authority, but often does so (and this is a fact to be carefully noted) actually in the context of its pronouncements on the hierarchy as service:

> Matthew 18:1ff., on the need to become as little children, begins a chapter entirely devoted to the ministry, with vv. 15–18 on excommunication for sins of scandal.
>
> In the very same *logion* in which he bids the apostles not to seek the first places, nor let themselves be called rabbi, as is the way of the scribes and Pharisees, Jesus makes an exception for the authority of those who still sit on the chair of Moses: "Do whatever they teach you and follow it" (Matt 23:2–3).
>
> Luke 22:25–27, on the greater being he who serves, is immediately followed by the passage concerning Peter, vv. 28–30.
>
> John 13 begins with "The Father had given all things into his hands."

It would be just as mistaken to think that the ideal of loving service eliminated all "power" as it would be dangerous to believe that authority in Christianity had reality or was defined *in the same way* as a juridical authority or a temporal power, with, as a kind of appendix, a moral obligation to exercise it in a spirit of service.

Unfortunately, this has too often been the case in the history of the Church, in particular, each time that the leaders of the Church have been involved in conflict with secular powers and have translated their reaction in terms of power against power: in Gregory VII's struggle against the Emperor Henry IV;[22] during the thirteenth century; in the struggles of bishops and popes against kings; at the time of the great quarrel between Boniface VIII and Philip the Fair, and so on. Against this background of purely juridical claims, even gospel texts on the pastorate have been used to justify the most flagrant examples of constraint.[23] The way in which biblical themes, which are fundamentally spiritual, have been translated into juridical terms makes a deplorable but highly instructive story.

In a more general way, ecclesiology has too often become simply a treatise on public ecclesiastical law. As one result of this, the Church gave up applying to herself the New Testament themes of conversion, of the war of the spirit against the flesh, etcetera (and indeed, given the conditions, this would have been impossible), although the ecclesiological passages of the fathers and the liturgy are full of such applications. The fathers never separate the "Church" and the community of the faithful; their ecclesiology is from beginning to end a Christian anthropology. But obviously a juridical institution, a power as such, or a legal structure, are not called on to be converted, nor to wage war against the flesh, nor to do penance, nor to practice humility, nor to forgive, nor to pray. In short, the domain of men and the Christian community was neglected for the domain of *things*.

The fourteenth and fifteenth centuries saw a slight reaction, but this was still within the juridical sphere, so that to reinstate the pope in his evangelical place as servant, there was erected a juridical theory of the *caput ministerial*; yet another theory of public law, contradicting the one that went before it but of the same kind. This was not the right reaction.

AS ONE OF YOU

We must get back to the true vision of the gospel: posts of authority in the Church do indeed exist; a real jurisdictional power does exist, which the shepherds of God's people receive from Christ in conformity with the order that Christ willed and instituted (at least in its essential lines). This power, however, exists only within the structure of the fundamental religious relationship of the gospel, as an organizational element within the life given to men by Christ, the one Lord and the one Head of his Body, for which each is accountable to all the rest according to the place and measure granted to him. So there is never simply a relationship of subordination or superiority, as in secular society, but always a loving obedience to Christ, shaping the life of each with all and for all, according to the position that the Lord has given him in the

Body. In this service, fundamentally identical and coextensive with the fact of being a Christian, some command and others obey: whether as leaders or as simple members of the brotherhood, they are wholly engaged in the service of Christ and their brethren.

> But speaking the truth in love, we must grow up in every way into him who is the head, into Christ, from whom the whole body, joined and knit together by every ligament with which it is equipped, as each part is working properly, promotes the body's growth in building itself up in love. (Eph 4:15–16)

The relationship of superiority and subordination is transformed by this. It is always of the Lord and in the Lord. Not only in the sense—which we know only too well from pronouncements designed to inculcate obedience—that subordinates must consider their superiors as representing God himself and bearing in their person the majesty of God, but in the sense that superiors and subordinates must serve God and men, confessing that all is God's grace for all and through all, according to the order in which God has placed each one of us. The superior has indeed a position of authority, but in a brotherly community of service: in the midst of the faithful he is *quasi unus ex illis*—"as one of them."[24]

All of this presupposes a radical conversion in us, not so much to an ethical ideal of disinterestedness, for such an ideal is only a consequence, but to God and Christ as the one absolute Lord: a conversion both *theistic* and *theological*. Much the same conversion as we must achieve if we are to "use [this world] as though not using it."[25] We must, in fact, sacrifice, abandon our human relationships in the form in which we receive them from the physical world of our first birth, which consist of two terms only: man and woman, master and servant, and we must receive them afresh from the hand of the Father as *Christian* relationships, and let them shape our lives "in the Lord," so that we live in the unique relationship of love of God, of Christ, and of men as God and Christ love them, or, better, of the very love with which God and Christ love them. "God so loved the world." Only after such conversion can the relationship of authority exist and be lived in a Christian fashion.

II

TITLES AND HONORS IN THE CHURCH

A SHORT HISTORICAL STUDY

1

THE INVASION OF LEGALISM

If we go to the fathers and the liturgy to discover what idea they had of the Church, we find ourselves in a climate that is not that of modern ecclesiology, at any rate not that of the ecclesiology predominant in the Schools between the end of the sixteenth century—or even the beginning of the fourteenth—and the renewal of our times. This scholastic ecclesiology was hardly more than the apologetic version of a treatise on public ecclesiastical law; it was entirely preoccupied with powers and rights. The fathers and the liturgy speak of the Church in terms of the life and fellowship of the spirit, of the Holy City, of the war of the spirit waged against the flesh. They see her as symbolized or typified by the patriarchs; by Rahab, the harlot saved by the scarlet cord tied in her window, which stands for faith in the blood of Christ; by Mary Magdalene, the unchaste one who became chaste; or by the Virgin Mary, blessed because she believed rather than because she bore Jesus Christ. For to them the Church is made up of all who are converted to the gospel. Their ecclesiology includes an anthropology and the means (sacraments, rules of life) by which men may live in communion with God in Jesus Christ.

A TURNING POINT:
THE GREGORIAN REFORM

This form of ecclesiology persisted into the early Middle Ages. The great Schoolmen were in general still faithful to this tradition. But by the end of the eleventh century, a new element was at work, a result of the Gregorian reform begun even before Gregory VII by Leo IX and Nicholas II. St. Leo IX, with the advice and encouragement of Humbert of Moyenmoutier, and after him, Gregory VII in particular, saw that the only possible way to effect the needful conversion of the clergy from the evils of the Nicolaitanism (incontinence) and even more from simony was to extricate the Church from her subjection to secular powers and, as a means to this end, to strengthen the authority and hence also the influence of the papacy. Gregory VII asked canonists, in the first place St. Peter Damian, to search out and assemble all the texts that could be used to support the strongest and most far-reaching form of papal authority and, under it, a wholesome order in the Church. Several canonical collections owe their existence to Gregory's appeal. It gave the decisive impetus to the establishment of canon law, alongside theology, as a discipline of university type in the schools, in the days when scholasticism was beginning; after St. Yves of Chartres, Gratian of Bologna, with his *Decretum* (1140), was the classic exponent of the new science.

With Roland Bandinelli, who became Alexander III (1159–81), canon law was firmly established on the pontifical throne. For two centuries thereafter, almost all popes were canonists, sometimes doctors in both Roman law and ecclesiastical law.

This ascendancy of canon law was a development that the papacy found particularly useful in its conflict with the secular powers that continued throughout the "age of faith": this was the age of "Christendom," when ideally the two powers were as the two arms of one body, the two "ministries" of a single Christian society. The main concern of the priesthood, or more accurately of the papacy, was to assert its rights in the face of a secular power ever ready to resist or encroach on them. *Ecclesia non est ancilla, sed domina*—"The Church is not a servant, but a mistress."[1] Gregory VII's words were spoken in the context of the pope's struggle against the Emperor Henry IV. It must be understood in relation to this historical context (the need to shake off the tutelage, if not the domination, of the temporal power), but it is nevertheless a disturbing statement, being in substance the direct opposite of the gospel principle: *non dominari, sed ministrare*, not to rule but to serve. Gregory VII and the Gregorians, for example, St. Anselm, made frequent use of the idea of the Church-Spouse, the Bride. Granted, this is definitely a mystical theme, but now directed—one might say slanted—toward an affirmation of the rights and authority of the "Church," that is, of clerics. As the Bride *of the Lord*, the Church is for all the faithful, but particularly for kings, "Mother and Mistress"— mistress above all; her motherhood is invoked only to support her authority. Movements, even policies, have the strength of their "mystique." In this case, the "mystique" of an entire faith gave extraordinary strength to the claims of the clergy to liberty, authority, and dominance. The story of St. Thomas Becket and his "murder in the cathedral" is an outstanding illustration of this.

THE ORIGINS OF THE TREATISE ON THE CHURCH

Ecclesiology began to be a subject treated in its own right with the works written in the thick of the struggle between the popes and the kings or emperors. The decisive moment in this connection was the conflict between Philip the Fair and Boniface VIII. In the space of a few months in 1300–1302 appeared the *De regimine christiano* of James of Viterbo, whose modern editor, H. X. Arquillière (1926), called it "the first treatise on the Church"; the *De ecclesiastica potestate* of Giles of Rome; the *De potestate papali et regali* of John of Paris; and others.

Furthermore, in the twenty years at the end of the thirteenth century and the first forty of the fourteenth, a legalistic form of reasoning overran whole sectors of theology. We feel the truth of this when we pass from reading St. Thomas Aquinas or St. Bonaventure, both of whom died in 1274 (one on his way to the Council of Lyons, the other while taking part in the council), to those of Henry of Ghent (d. 1293), for example, and above all William of Occam (d. 1349–50). Theological positions and conclusions were determined not so much by inherent reasons, arrived at after contemplative consideration of the deep inner nature of things, as by purely positive authorities, decretal texts the strength of whose coercive value was carefully assessed. On the subject of realities, an attitude based on consideration of normality yielded to a damaging approach, by way of exceptional cases, possible dispensations, and the most far-fetched hypotheses. Nominalism was voluntarist; it was concerned with what God can do in extreme cases, regardless of what is reasonable (dialectic of the *potentia absoluta*, as opposed to the *potentia ordinata*). It resulted in a kind of positivism of free choice, which encourages fideism in those who remain within the Church, or else a certain skepticism.

In theology, ethics, liturgy, and the like, legalism raises the question of the most positive and strict conditions in which a thing can still bear its own name, be valid, and satisfy an obligation. This attitude was especially prevalent and destructive in the liturgy.[2] Here it fostered an old material and markedly unspiritual instinct, which led men to concern themselves with the rite, the material and obligatory aspect of what was required of them, and not with the deeply personal involvement of the man who is not content merely to pay a debt but pledges his heart; interest was focused on the minimum legal conditions of validity necessary for compliance with the law, at least with the letter of the law and authority, and not on the *meaning* of things. A similar attitude of mind, in matters of human conduct, resulted in the conception of casuistry as the art of getting round the law while respecting the letter of it.[3]

THE SPIRITUAL DEGRADED INTO "THINGS"

In all these cases, we see living spiritual reality, inner quality, and personal involvement degraded into *things*. A whole study could be devoted to this process of degradation in the pastoral letter, which can so easily degenerate into a series of recipes, a letter devoted to "things." There is much, too, to be written about "moralism," of which it has been said, "Moralism begins at the point where the action is considered more important than the inspiration from which it springs."[4] Good and evil are then detached, as it were, from the living subject that embraces them and for which they qualify, and considered as things to be defined quantitatively by reference to completely external standards. Man is subordinated to the Sabbath, not the Sabbath to man. Regulation of a thing goes beyond the service necessary for good order and becomes a value in itself. I have shown elsewhere[5] how the treatise of the Church took shape first in a climate of strife between the two powers and their respective claims, then in a climate of refutation of successive heresies: the conciliarist heresy that refused to acknowledge the force of the papal element in the Church's divine constitution; the heresy of Wycliffe and Huss (Church of the Elect), which cast doubts on the visible nature of the Church and her hierarchical structure; the heresies of the Protestant reformers, who added to Wycliffe's a radical denial of the priesthood, the power of bishops and the pope, the sacraments, and so on; the heresies of the Gallicans and the episcopalist movement, which diminished the authority of the pope. All of these heresies pointed in much the same direction. The reaction of orthodoxy followed their lead; it emphasized the aspects of the hierarchy, ending up by seeing the Church as practically nothing more than a society in which some commanded and the rest obeyed, but above all, it exalted authority. It considered the Church from the viewpoint of her rights and the powers that made her a social structure; in a word, as a juridical subject of authority and rights.

Correspondingly, the relations of the Church with the world were seen chiefly from the legal standpoint, the main theme being the question of the two *Powers*. True, the deep inward life of the Church was constantly at work correcting and balancing these unilateral tendencies. On the one hand, the Church was still the Church of the saints, of the life of the gospel, of the love of God and man: "Our Church is the Church of the saints" (G. Bernanos); she was still the Church of prayer, celebrating the liturgy and keeping safe within it, as in a living casket, the treasure of her deep-rooted tradition. On the other hand, she was intensely apostolic and missionary, as she must always be for her full health. Furthermore, it was very largely the hierarchy itself that effectively encouraged, by constant exhortation, the apostolate, the spirit of mission, charity, and prayer, and kept safe the liturgy and the rules of holy life.

There is nothing whatsoever in my observations to suggest that the Church of charity and the Church of law are in any way opposed. All I have done is to explain historically how legalism has crept (as I am sure it has) into the outward appearances of the Church and sometimes into her practice. What I have criticized is a certain way of envisaging and presenting the Church; we must keep what truth it contains, but we must denounce as an evil, from which the contemporary Church is, moreover, recovering remarkably quickly, its tyrannical and unworthy claims to ascendancy.

2

HOW THE CHURCH HAS ACQUIRED ITS APPEARANCE OF PRIVILEGE

Before I approach the question of honors in the Church (insignia and titles) historically, I must explain why I feel it to be a matter of considerable importance. Honors are by no means a negligible element in the Church's visible structure, and this is not only theologically a very important characteristic but also one of decisive importance in practical affairs. It is by the outward signs of the Church, by what she is seen to be, that men know her and through her are, or should be, brought to the gospel, led to God, or else they are estranged from her, repelled or even turned toward some sort of religion of material things, a system where sociological conduct predominates, rather than toward a personal religion with its inherent spiritual demands. From this point of view, then, the greatest importance attaches to everything that makes the Church visible, everything by which it comes into contact with men's lives, as their faces, looks, shape, and outward trappings give us contact with our fellows; it may be the wording of a poster, a notice, a parish magazine, or more likely a form of ornamentation or celebration, the look of the priest, his manner or turn of speech, the way he lives—and the same applies to a nun, or any cleric. These are minor everyday elements in the Church's visible form, in her role as the parable of the kingdom of God or the sacrament of the gospel, but they have their significance nonetheless and it may be decisive. The average person comes across the leaders and dignitaries of the Church less frequently, but the image of the Church they present is obviously just as important—even more important, as their appearances are likely to be more memorable.

On the other hand, our outward circumstances, the setting in which we live our lives, the way we are customarily treated, the image of ourselves and our office that we see reflected in all of these, are powerful factors in molding our ideas and attitude. Can we as a rule enjoy privileges without coming to feel they are rights; live in some degree of luxury without forming certain habits; be honored, flattered, treated with solemn and brilliant ceremonial without setting ourselves morally on a pedestal? Can we always command and judge, receive men as petitioners, eager with their compliments, without getting into the habit of not really listening? In short, if we are always attended by thurifers, can we avoid acquiring a liking for incense?

INSIGNIA AND TITLES

Among the aspects of privilege in the Church's image in the world today, I shall confine myself here to insignia and titles. First, because I must set myself a limit; a study of all that goes to make the Church's visible aspect would be too extensive. Then because insignia and titles, especially the former, have been the subject of a great many studies in the last thirty years, especially by German historians, who are very much alive (sometimes excessively so) to what concerns the Holy Roman Empire and, in consequence, to this aspect of ecclesiastical realities.

Modern historians of apostolic and primitive Christianity reject the idea that the first Christian communities existed without any definite juridical organization. The historical evidence—the Letters, the Acts, the letters of St. Clement of Rome and of St. Ignatius of Antioch ("Theophorus"), the Epistle and the Martyrdom of St. Polycarp, and finally the *Didache* whose date and provenance are so elusive—all show a very real authority at the head of the Churches. But this was an authority of leaders outstanding in spiritual gifts, of leaders of the spiritual life; the juridical domain did not extend to matters of spiritual warfare, or the ecclesiological to the affairs of man as a spiritual and Christian being. The prestige of the leaders of God's people stood high, but we have no evidence that they used external means to support it.

Yet it is only human to use such means. Even before the peace of Constantine, we see signs of a tendency to seek prestige through external, honorific distinctions. Paul of Samosata had a high throne set up for himself, and the bishops had to appeal to the Emperor Aurelian (a pagan!) before they could dispossess him of his see of Antioch.[1] But in the new situation created by Constantine, external means of prestige were introduced as the result not of men's natural instincts alone but of the new conditions imposed on the Church within the Empire.

THE CHURCH WITHIN THE EMPIRE

Although we must not lay all evils at the door of Constantine the Great, we must recognize the influence of his policy on conditions of life in the Church. Henceforward the Church was *within the Empire*, as Optatus of Milevis wrote about 370.[2] The Bishop of Milevis, confronted with the Donatist schism, resorted to the logic of the age that began with Constantine; he claimed recourse to force and to State compulsion to be justifiable, in order to crush stubborn dissentients and those who foment sedition.[3]

Under Constantine and after his time, in the framework of an officially Christian Empire, the bishops were given privileges and honors. They ranked in the Order of the *Illustri* and took their place in the hierarchy of the State. Men who were in hiding the very day before, some bearing the marks of tortures undergone during the persecution, travelled to the Council of Nicaea (325) by the imperial post, and as they came out of the council were received in the Imperial Palace at Constantinople, honored by the highest officials. "It felt," wrote Eusebius, "as if we were transported into the Kingdom of God."[4]

It is difficult to be sure of the exact origin of different insignia and difficult to say definitely that they began in a borrowing from the official dress of the great imperial officers. But this does seem to have been the case with the *pallium*, which made its appearance in both East and West in the fifth century, and with the *stola* and the pontifical shoes, which date from the same period and were the insignia of high officials. Certainly, priests were put on their guard against the dangers of secularization and loss of savor that the favors of the political authorities represented for Christianity and the Church.[5] But how could such favors be avoided? The privileges accorded to the clergy could easily be justified by the argument that they served spiritual and heavenly realities far higher than all the earthly realities that were honored. Moreover, the liturgy, hitherto sober and functional, content to express the spiritual worship of the faith in acts of acceptance of God's gift and of thanksgiving, now began to develop a splendid ceremonial, many of its elements being borrowed from that of the court: processions, sumptuous vestments, gold furnishings and vessels—all the rich display of liturgical ceremonies.

It became natural to use a vocabulary originating in the imperial or political sphere in speaking of the realities of Christianity: the gospel is a "law"; God is the supreme Emperor of the world, and the angels his ministers; Peter and Paul are the *principes* (princes) or *senatores mundi* (high dignitaries of the world).[6]

So there came to be added to the sacred things of God himself, which are the realities at work in the history of salvation, which men gladly receive and use, the sacred things of a ceremonial of great beauty, rich in symbols that the contemplative soul will never exhaust, to its unfailing joy. For example, in primitive days, churches were consecrated only by the congregation's habitual use, and the fact of a first Eucharist celebrated on the altar, but from the fourth century, there was introduced a sanctification and consecration of the altar before this first celebration, in a rite taken from the Old Testament. In our day, the consecration of churches has developed into a ceremony that is full of wonderful symbolism, but complicated and spectacular, involving a ritual consecration of *things*, which tends to swamp the sanctification of the *Ecclesia* by living faith.

VESTIGES OF FEUDALISM

The history whose great epochs and main elements I am trying to define reached its first peak in the centuries that saw the peace of Constantine and the establishment of the legislative code of the Most Christian Empire (Theodosius), followed by the conversion of barbarian princes and the setting up of Christian kingdoms. Its second great period, in the West, came at the end of the Merovingian and into the Carolingian age. Germanic influence, very pronounced at that time, led to the meaning of everything that was done being translated into gestures, by handing over and touching a significant object; for example, to pledge obedience one put one's hands between the hands of a superior; investiture involved the tradition of the instruments or insignia. It is in Visigothic Spain in the seventh century, in Gaul in the eighth, that we first find the crozier, or at least the pastoral staff (*baculus*, *virga*). This was unknown in Rome before the eleventh century, although the Bishop of Rome appears in the eighth century bearing a *ferula* (pastoral staff). The episcopal ring appears in the eighth century in Spain and Gaul.

Much more important at this time was the revival of the idea, the prestige, and the ideal of the Empire and Rome as a reality or myth of empire. Possibly, it sprang from the need to compete with Byzantium, whence genuflection (*proskunesis*) and the kissing of feet were borrowed at that time; possibly from the desire to make a stand against Frankish influence, at once protective and intrusive. Historians are still arguing over the date, place of composition, and exact intention of the all too famous "Donation of Constantine." However important these details may be, they do not affect the results that concern us here: all things considered, the legendary "Donation," which was almost everywhere accepted as authentic down to the time of the humanists (Lorenzo Valla), and was still invoked by some nineteenth-century ultra-montanists, had considerable influence on the tendency to model the realities of the Church on the realities of the Empire. We will not concern ourselves here with the ideological myth of an Empire that was to endure forever, and of one universal republic united under the aegis of some supreme power.[7] It was thought that Constantine had been warned by a vision of the apostles Peter and Paul to seek out Pope

Sylvester, and had been baptized and cured of leprosy by him. He had then resolved to honor the pope, vicar of the Son of God on earth, he who occupied the place of the prince of apostles, by bestowing on him the authority and honors of the imperial dignity.[8] The rest of the document deals with the Lateran Church, *caput et vertex* (head and pinnacle) of all churches,[9] the Lateran Palace,[10] and then the imperial insignia conceded to the pope: the diadem, the *phrygium* (but it is said that Sylvester would accept only the round white miter, the *phrygium*, and not the diadem), the shoulder scarf, the purple cloak (*chlamys*), the red tunic—in short, all the adornments of an emperor, even down to the scepter; it is clear from the text that the imperial character of these insignia was well understood.[11] The pope, like the emperor, was to have his senate and his legates; there are of course biblical antecedents for these (councils, messengers), but they make their appearance here as institutions modeled on those of the Empire.[12] The emperor was to exercise the *officium statoris* (the office of squire) as Constantine did, leading on foot the horse on which the pope rode. There follows the well-known gift of lands *ad imitationem Imperii nostri* (modeled on our Empire),[13] and finally the statement that Constantine has seen fit to transfer his capital to the East.[14]

These authorizations had far-reaching effect. Not that the popes themselves invoked the legendary Donation—that would have been an admission that they owed something to the concession of a secular power, and they were conscious that they held their authority by right of the gospel and by divine right itself. But the imperial idea, upheld by all the concrete apparatus of insignia, titles, the organization of the Roman court and its services, in a word, all the ceremonial, was largely responsible for the development of papal claims and the day-to-day administration of the Church along imperial lines. Representations, images, and myths were all those of a monarchy on the imperial model. So were all the appendages of prestige. In more than one case, tracing these external signs of sovereignty back through history, we are led beyond Byzantium to the time of the Hellenistic monarchy, and it even seems that this derived several of its insignia from Persia.

The Church lives in time. The structures, ideas, and means of action existing in a historical setting at a given moment largely condition the outward forms of her life and action. For more than half a millennium, the Church lived among feudal structures, and from this time date many of the texts on which Catholic theology has been built up. Feudalism was a social system determined by two facts: (1) every man was bound to the land and his condition was determined by that of the land on which he was born and lived, and (2) lands were not equal in value.

Under the feudal system, a man was always bound to the land, and the land transmitted its value to the man living on it; he was lord, landowner and master, or vassal and tenant, according to whether he possessed the land or held it from another in return for certain duties or services. These relations extended hierarchically from top to bottom of society, from the king who was no one's dependent but to whom the lords were enfeoffed, down to the poor man who was simply a dependent, the liegeman of a lord who was himself the liegeman of his suzerain. The Church too was subject to this system. Although her lands were gradually freed and made directly subject to the king, she too had her vassals and tenants; she too had a hierarchy of nobles, linked with the lands attached to certain offices; she had bishops who were princes or counts;[15] she had chapters and abbeys varying in degree of dignity. In this medieval, hierarchical world, a man's quality, which included his duties and rights, his obligations and privileges, was expressed not only in titles and insignia but in a manner of living, a style of dress. Today, when things of quality can be bought and are available to anyone who can pay for them, anyone can wear any clothes. But dress proper to a calling or condition still persists, even though the feudal system has long since been swept away, and to some extent maintains a distinction of orders, for example, in army and clergy, and in each uniforms and insignia of rank. No doubt this will be so for a long time yet.

It is important for our discussion to recognize that the feudal age has left traces behind it. We can attach what importance we like to them. *Dominus* carries little weight in "Dom" So-and-so, and "Monsignor" is no less inoffensive. Titles such as "my Lord Bishop" are, or should be, the province of local history societies, together with old titles vested in chapters, which only rarely survive nowadays and are reflected in a few details of costume. Feudalism is a thing of the past. Yet surely there still clings about bishops and the Curia an aura of feudal privilege expressed in dress, insignia, "retinue,"[16] the deference paid to them,[17] all the trappings of heraldry? The economic and social structures of feudalism have disappeared, but some vestiges remain on the surface, and occasionally titles and privileges still have some real value, but they are mainly external, part of the nature of man in his physical state.

CONSTANTINE OR PETER?

The third great period of extensive borrowings of titles and insignia from the powers of this world was during the reforming pontificate of St. Gregory VII (1073–85). The facts are all before us, in the chronicles, the *Ordines Romani* describing the ceremonies of the pope's coronation and enthronement, the *realia*, the monuments that have survived to our days. But we also have most explicit statements: in particular, the *Dictatus Papae*, the list of propositions drawn up by Gregory VII in 1075, which represent the legal basis of the claims he wished to see maintained. Here are some of them: *Quod solus [Papa] possit uti imperialihus insigniis* (Only the pope is entitled to use the imperial insignia);[18] the corresponding passage in the Avranches manuscript reads, *Soli Papae licet in processionibus insigne quod vocatur regnum portare cum reliquo paratu imperiali* (Only the pope may wear in processions the insignia known as the tiara, or the rest of the imperial insignia) (c. 10). What were these insignia? First the red cloak and the red shoes, introduced as early as the eighth century. Then the tiara, *corona* or *regnum*, a triple-ringed miter distinct from the ordinary miter (in the mid-eleventh century the word *mitra* began to be used for the old *phrygium*), which was called the *tiara* from the end of the eleventh century onward. The Church was well aware that it was imitating the Empire or the structure of Ancient Rome. It was then that the cardinals, who elected the pope without any intervention of laymen, were assimilated to the senate of the Church, and that the word *curia* was introduced to designate the services of the pontifical administration and the pope's entourage.[19] Soon afterward St. Bernard repudiated the term as a neologism and an indication that secular usages were invading the Church.[20]

It was St. Bernard too who wrote to his former subordinate Pope Eugenius III (r. 1145–53): "When the pope, clad in silk, covered with gold and jewels, rides out on his white horse, escorted by soldiers and servants, he looks more like Constantine's successor than St. Peters's."[21] St. Bernard likewise censured the pomp that surrounded bishops, covered with red-dyed ermine "called gules";[22] they look like young brides on their wedding day![23] And he upbraided the abbots who had just then obtained from the Holy See the right to wear a miter, ring, and sandals, like the bishops.[24]

The fourth epoch in the history whose most significant stages we are reviewing was the reign of Boniface VIII (1294–1303), a man whose character allows of conflicting interpretations. It was he who introduced the triple tiara, the *triregnum*, which can be seen on the head of St. Peter's statue in the majestic nave of the Vatican Basilica. The shape of the tiara, rising from a wide base to a single point at the top, was an apt expression of the idea of pontifical monarchy and a quasi-pyramidal concept of the Church. The triple-crowned tiara symbolizes the unity of the Church extending over a united world: the true ecumenical emperor is the pope, he who rules over the unity of the universe. It was inevitable that conflict should arise between the old imperial idea of universal unity under a single crowned head, and the papal idea, which based its claim to be the means of effecting this grandiose program on the most sacred grounds. In the course of their rivalry, however, both empire and papacy borrowed the other's ideological themes, translated into physical or symbolic terms.

To the pomp of Renaissance times, we owe many of the forms of ceremonial and protocol used today by the papal court.

Borrowing on both sides continued. Nowadays, abuse of the printed word, and notably journalism, has atrociously weakened the meaning of language, and only the vocabulary of religion still keeps its force and prestige. So we resort to it when we want to express things on a certain level of intensity or dignity. The order of religion still has great prestige. We speak of a sufferer as a martyr to his illness, medicine or teaching is a *vocation* and so on.[25] But the Church also borrows terms: after taking over the Byzantine title of "Eminence," she has in our own time adopted the title of "Excellency," so that no less honor may be imputed to her bishops than Mussolini allowed his prefects.

"SHAKE OFF THE DUST OF THE EMPIRE"

The modern state has reviewed and largely rejected its borrowings from the Church, and that admixture of sacred or religious elements, which for centuries it not only admitted but sought out. The tendency of modern society is to build on reason, not on religion.[26] Has the Church likewise reviewed the profane elements, imperial, feudal, or courtly, which for so long she not only tolerated but actively encouraged? The Holy Roman Empire no longer exists, but there remain in the Church many titles and insignia, many elements of ceremonial and so of her visible aspect, borrowed at some time from the dazzling imperial splendor. Surely it is high time and surely it would be to everyone's advantage "to shake off the dust of the Empire that has gathered since Constantine's day on the throne of St. Peter." Those words were spoken by John XXIII.

In time past, these trappings, this whole system of symbols, developed a meaning, which in that social tradition, was readily understandable even to the humblest. Such is no longer the case today. In one sense, this is a good thing, since it makes them relatively inoffensive. Nevertheless, even if their exact import is no longer clearly apparent, they still carry a general implication of external, worldly, feudal, imperial prestige. Though they no longer have definite positive value, they have the general value of symbols, and what they express is not that evangelical service to which the very men who bear these insignia and titles of a different world are dedicated (often with very great fervor). There has been much talk recently of "countersigns." We must ask ourselves, in the light of the gospel, what are the consequences or effects of all these signs of prestige.

It is not an easy problem. We must have signs and insignia. When the highest office is borne by a man too much like other men, perhaps even less well-favored or well-endowed than they, his person must, as it were, be set free from the too personal, too human limits of his individuality, and in some way, exalted and honored by the badges of his dignity.

The possibilities in this direction are limited—a few fabrics, a few colors, forms of honorific headgear or long flowing garments to add splendor and nobility. Once again, it must be acknowledged that the Church has in general succeeded in creating honorific forms of great and compelling beauty. Fr. Romane-Musculus recently argued in favor of an official dress that gives a man impersonality and focuses attention on his office, but he was talking of liturgical vestments. I am myself unreservedly in favor not only of liturgical vestments, but of a dress expressing state or office, of insignia interpreting the dignity and inspiring respect for it. But all of this must be (1) intelligible and more in keeping with the world we live in; (2) less weighted, or over-weighted, with history to the point where certain things need research and erudite footnotes to explain them; and (3) always commensurate with the office, which, in the last resort, means with service, and that implies a drastic revision of everything stemming from dignities, situations, and sometimes pretentions that are secular and political and have very little to do with the gospel.

It is not easy to say exactly what we should like to see changed. Perhaps indeed we ought not to try to change things too quickly. We must state the problem, collect information that will throw light on the admitted facts, foster a healthy insistence on the truth of the gospel in this sphere as in others, and then leave the Christian people and their priests to find valid ways to meet this need for truth and authenticity. I shall end this contribution, which has been on the level of a historical investigation and a few questions of principle, by suggesting some reflections of greater scope than the particular problem of titles and insignia we have broached here.

In antiquity and the Middle Ages, there were few images of beauty and luxury and splendor apart from those of temples and palaces, priests and kings. The need for something that went beyond the commonplace, something that kindled and sustained the imagination, found almost its only satisfaction in the splendid pageantry of princes and religious ceremonies, and in the legends of saints, which did much to meet this human need for something more than the humdrum daily round. When the Russians, who were still not highly civilized, went to Byzantium and witnessed the splendid Greek liturgy, they thought themselves in heaven: "We knew not if we were in heaven or on earth, for there is no such spectacle on earth, nor any such beauty."[27]

Today, pomp and splendor can be found outside the churches. These elements undoubtedly contribute to the attraction of dance halls and cinemas. It is true, though, that by comparison, church ceremonies have a dignity, perfection and beauty, an emotional quality of reverence, that cannot be equaled by any other ceremonial. A friend who is very "lay," even a little anticlerical, once said to me, "It is only in church nowadays that ceremony can be properly performed."

Above all, our imagination today has more to feed on than the mysteries of the liturgy or the legends of the saints. Indeed, modern man's imagination is in danger of being overfed: novels, daily papers, magazines, cinemas, television....But it has a still more exciting and certainly healthier outlet in the endless perspectives opened up by scientific discoveries. The Crusades did much to create a new humanity, more enterprising and already eager for freedom. The voyages and great discoveries of the late fifteenth century helped to awaken a new man, fascinated by his own powers, the man of the Renaissance, and modern man is the grandson of the voyages, enterprises, research, and achievements of the nineteenth century. We can hardly doubt that a new humanity will be born of the inventions and discoveries of today. Wide horizons open before modern man. For him, the attraction of the Church will lie not in miraculous hagiography or ceremonial splendor, but far more in the truth he finds in her of the spiritual relationship of communion with others—a relationship founded on the genuine and exacting gospel attitude of living faith, inward obedience, true prayer, love, and service. God's beacons on the threshold of the atomic age are Thérèse of Lisieux, Charles de Foucauld, the Little Brothers and Little Sisters, and their counterparts at Taizé. Our nonreligious age is also the age of a surprising revival of evangelism. Men want the truth of the gospel, its authenticity and simplicity, and on those conditions, they are ready to accept its demands ungrudgingly. We can no longer hope to dazzle men with purple and gold, heraldry and titles ending in "-issimus." He compels us now to show forth in our lives the truth of what we profess to believe and love with all our heart.

Who can complain of that?

III

BY
WAY OF
CONCLUSION

am very conscious of the inadequacy of these few pages in comparison with the holy cause announced in my title. I have been able to approach only from afar, from the outside, and from one particular angle the problem (or rather the mystery) of a Church imbued with the gospel ideal of poverty. God willing, and granting me courage and strength for the undertaking, I would wish one day to put forward in all humility some reflections on what is the basis of the biblical attitude of faith, and the very heart of the Beatitudes: "Blessed are the poor in spirit!"

Everything that I have said so far shows that several styles have followed one another in the Church's visible presence in the world. No single formula can exhaust the relations of the spiritual with the temporal; none of the forms taken by these relations fully expresses the reality of a Church whose substance escapes time, being of different order from the things of this world. The Church makes full use of the possibilities that history offers her to live and work in the world, but because she is not of the world, she reserves the right to lay aside what has served her for a season and to use other means or give other expression to her life.

Nowadays, she is called on to find a new style for her presence in the world. A presence founded on prestige, exercising an authority whose superiority was acknowledged even on the level of law, may have been acceptable, and indeed required in an age of unanimity in religion. When no other voice but the Church's taught men how they should walk, no other arm but hers upheld them, they accepted her not only as the messenger of Jesus Christ but, within the structure of society on this earth and at the very apex of its social organization, as an authority endowed with privileges, splendor, and the means of action that befitted her station. But now men have taken over the ordering of the affairs of the world and become so engrossed by them that they can no longer find interest for anything else. The world has lost the spiritual unity of ancient Christendom; it is divided, and its divisions are in all probability final. Moreover, increased production of the means of comfortable living involves men in such relentless competition, intricate organization, and stimulation of appetites and compulsions that even as they become kings, they are in danger of losing the health that was theirs in a less affluent and exalted position.

Confronting this world, or rather surrounded by it, the Church finds herself in a situation that must be recognized not only as one historical situation among others, neither better nor worse than others, but also that conforms much more closely with the law of the gospel. She is called on to make a clean break with the old forms of her presence in the world, legacies from the days when she controlled the hand that bore the scepter, and to find a new style of being present to men. Individual initiative and spearhead groups that have made their appearance in every country have already clearly outlined the shape of this new style. Now it must be given recognition, some sort of consecration on the scale of the universal Church, and urged in the strongest terms at the next session of the Council.

I was able to say that the present situation of the Church is in closer conformity with the law of Christian life first, because of the distinction and tension between the Church and the world, which was weakened, if not effaced, by the regime of Christendom. And by the same reasoning, because she has been freed from the dangers of an association or symbiosis with temporal society that tempted the clergy to adopt the attitudes of the world, not to be ashamed to speak the language of the world or to wear the world's tawdry livery of tinsel and gilt. In a world that has become, or has become again, purely "worldly," the Church finds herself forced, if she would still be anything at all, to be simply the Church, witness to the gospel and the kingdom of God, through Jesus Christ and in view of him. That is what men need, and that is what they expect of her. In fact, if we listed all their most valid claims on the Church, we should find that they amounted to this: that she be less *of* the world and more *in* the world; that she be simply the Church of Jesus Christ, the conscience of men in the light of the gospel, but that she be this with her whole heart.

The characteristics of this style of her presence in conformity with the gospel are outlined in the Acts of the Apostles and the writings of the New Testament. They can be reduced to three terms, compact with the greatest possible spiritual meaning: *koinonia, diakonia, marturia* (fellowship, service, witness). The World Council of Churches has made these three terms the foundation, as it were the tripod on which its program of action stands, and by so doing has gone straight to the heart of truth in its most authentic form. Every initiative inspired by the gospel leads instinctively in this direction. The ground has been so well prepared, so many appeals are being made to us, that this is the moment for the whole Church to find the new style of her presence in the world by establishing, nourishing, and inspiring true communities of brothers, projects and associations for service, and acts of witness.

These three supreme realities could be the starting point of a positive program of Christian life in the world. The demands they make would not only affect individuals, but the Church herself, *qua* Church, and hence at the ecclesiological level. These three are the sure guides to Christian life, but what part have they in our treatises on the Church? To read them, it seems as if the Church could very well do without Christians and without the life of the gospel.

A positive program of this kind entails examination of various forms or attitudes that may in some degree betray the Church. To be honest, we are often more sinned against than sinning in our acceptance of these. We come into an inheritance not lacking in grandeur and titles of respect, but which is now so archaic, rigid, and ponderous that we risk being incapable of being *to men* what men themselves and what the gospel require us to be today. In the outward forms we have inherited from a venerable past, we must be ruthless critics of anything that may, on the one hand, betray the spirit of the gospel, and on the other, of anything that may isolate us and set up a barrier between us and men. Certain forms of prestige, certain titles or insignia, a certain protocol, certain ways of life and dress, an abstract and pompous vocabulary are all structures that isolate us, just as there are structures that humiliate or degrade. What was formerly in place in a world much more stable than ours and imbued with respect for established honors is today only a sure way to isolation: a barrier to what we most sincerely desire to express and communicate. Forms designed to inspire respect, to surround us with an aura of mystery, still persist, and their effect today is the opposite of what one would wish. Not only do they keep men at a distance from us, they keep us at a distance from men, so that the real world of their life is morally inaccessible to us. This is extremely serious. It means that we are, in fact, no longer able to meet men on the ground where they are most themselves, where they express themselves freely, experience their most real sorrows and joys, face their true problems. We are in danger of living in their midst, separated from them by a haze of fiction.

Naturally, our effort should reach down to include spiritual habits or images that themselves depend, at a still deeper level, on the ecclesiology that we profess at least in practice. We are still a long way from reaping the consequences of the rediscovery, which we have all made in principle, of the fact that the whole Church is a single people of God and that she is made up of the faithful as well as the clergy. We have an idea, we feel, implicitly and without admitting it, even unconsciously that the "Church" is the clergy and that the faithful are only our clients or beneficiaries. This terrible concept has been built into so many of our structures and habits that it seems to be taken for granted and beyond change. It is a betrayal of the truth. A great deal remains to be done to declericalize our conception of the Church (without, of course, jeopardizing her hierarchical structure), and to put the clergy back where they truly belong, in the place of member-servants. Much remains to be done before we can pass from the simple moral plane where as individuals we act in the spirit of humility and service, albeit within structures of caste and privilege, to the plane of ecclesiological concepts. According to St. Paul, ordained ministers in the Church are the joints or nerves on which the whole of the active body relies for its smooth working (see Eph 4:16). Their role is "the perfecting of the saints" (that is, of the faithful) "for the work of ministry" that is laid upon us all, whose end is the building up of the Body of Christ (v. 12).

We are still a long way from the goal!

To help us make the readjustments that are needed, to give us better understanding of what is at stake, to point the way to new forms of expression and presence in the world, nothing can be more useful than frank exchange of views between the Church and the world, between the Church and other Christians, and within the Church between clergy and laity, circumference and center, parish priests and theologians or specialists in the different disciplines that have something to contribute on this problem. It is in discussion that each finds the truth of his existence; it is the pooling of resources that gives the impetus needed to meet all the demands of one's personal convictions. For the Church, as for every one of us, health consists not only in being herself, but in working out in her life the truth of her relationship with others. A Church thus open to free discussion will be a Church of poverty and service too, a Church that has the word of the gospel to give to men: less *of* the world and more *for* the world!

IV

APPENDIX

OUR PASTORS SPEAK OF THE
CHURCH OF POVERTY AND SERVICE:
PASSAGES FROM THE COUNCIL,
THE POPE, AND THE BISHOPS

1

A
CHURCH
OF SERVICE

We, therefore, the followers of Christ, are not estranged from earthly concerns and toils. Indeed, the faith, hope and charity of Christ urges us to serve our brothers in imitation of the example of the Divine Master who "has not come to be served, but to serve" (Matt. 20:28).

Neither was the Church born, therefore, to dominate but to serve. "...He laid down His life for us; and we likewise ought to lay down our life for the brethren" (1 John 3:16). (*Message to the World of the Second Vatican Council*, October 20, 1962)

Our endeavor throughout these four years of humble service—as we understand it, and shall understand it to the end—has been that of the "servant of the servants" of God, who is in very truth the "Lord and Prince of Peace"....

The Council has watched the sense of unity unfolding like a flower, spontaneously, and in a way almost unexpected by most of us: the sense of unity, or rather of conscious, recognized and welcome attraction towards

Christian brotherhood, which is expressed in the Apostles' Creed by the compelling affirmation of the one holy Catholic and apostolic Church, made not to rule but to serve the nations, among whom Christ's design finds an answer in a yearning which is sincere, even if its extent and developments are not always entirely understood. (John XXIII, *Christmas Message*, 1962)

The lamb led to the slaughter opened not his mouth before his persecutors; in his death he reveals to us the secret of true fecundity.

May this law find its response in the hearts of all who bear responsibility for the rising generation: parents and teachers and all those who, being vested with authority, must regard themselves as being at the service of their brethren. May it be a special invitation, in the harmony of obedience, brotherly discipline, and common aspirations, to all who labor to spread through the world the light of the Gospel, the reflection of Christ's resurrection. (John XXIII, *Easter Message*, 1963)

Just because we have been raised to the highest level of the hierarchical scale of the power that is at work in the Church militant, we feel that at the same time we have been appointed to the most lowly office of servant of the servants of God. Authority and responsibility, honor and humility, right and duty, power and love, are thereby wonderfully united. We are mindful of the warning of Christ, whose vicar we have been appointed: "The greatest among you must become like the youngest, and the leader like one who serves" (Luke 22:26). (Paul VI, *Coronation Homily*, June 30, 1963)

Let us see the Church as *mater amabilis*, a mother to be loved. If papal primacy were presented to us as meaning first in service, and as the response to the three-fold question of love Christ put to Peter, it would be a language that all Christians, and even non-Christians understand. (Georges Hakim, Bishop of Akka (Melkite Greek), Israel, *Documentation Catholique*, 1963, col. 56, p. 5)

Their ordination has to some extent "set aside" priests to exercise an office of public authority in the Christian community. And as in the Church all authority is service, they are ordained as "servants" of their brethren, the laity: they kindle and sustain your faith, and keep ever at your disposal the light and strength you have need of, the Word of Christ and his divine life. (Gérard-Maurice-Eugène Huyghe, Bishop of Arras, *Pastoral Letter to the Laity of his Diocese*, Christmas 1962)

To have authority in the Church does not mean to rule, but to serve the welfare of the faithful. The Savior said of himself, "The Son of Man came not to be served but to serve, and to give his life a ransom for many" (Matt 20:28). In the same way the ministry of priests and bishops does not mean domination, but service, *ministerium,* as the pope makes clear in his traditional reference to himself as the Servant of the Servants of God, *Servus servorum Dei.* (Josef Cardinal Frings, Archbishop of Cologne, *Lenten Pastoral Letter*, 1963)

The first of the Gospel values: authority seen not as domination, but as *service.* "I am not come to be ministered unto, but to *minister!*"—the Lord's words recur again and again in what the Fathers have said at the Council. But not only a handful of bishops speak thus. The message of the Council Fathers to the world returned to it once more and added: *"That is why the Church is made not to rule, but to serve."* This expression is Pope Pius XII's. It is a straight answer to one of the most serious and frequent accusations levelled by the enemies of the Church against her power and her wish for dominion over States and peoples. It is an exacting program for her leaders: *to serve their people*. (Emile Maurice Guerry, Archbishop of Cambrai, *Pastoral Letter*, 1963).

2

A
CHURCH
OF POVERTY

Confronted by the underdeveloped countries, the Church presents herself as she is and wants to be: the Church of all men, and in particular the Church of the poor. (John XXIII, *Message to the Christian Faithful One Month before the Opening of the Council*, September 11, 1962)

We shall not meet the truest and deepest demands of our times, we shall not answer the hope of unity shared by all Christians, if we do no more than make the preaching of the Gospel to the poor one of the many themes of the Council. In fact it is not *a* theme; it is in some measure *the* theme of our Council. If, as has often been repeated here, it is true to say that the aim of this Council is to bring the Church into closer conformity with the truth of the Gospel and to fit her better to meet the problems of our day, we can say that the central theme of this Council is the Church precisely in so far as she is the Church of the poor. (Giacomo Cardinal Lercaro, Archbishop of Bologna, *Documentation Catholique*, March 3, 1963, col. 321, n. 2)

The Church must find again an aspect that has become a little blurred through the centuries: the look of poverty. Remembering that the apostles were no more than humble Galilean fishermen and that the Lord himself was pleased to live in poverty, she will strive to be more completely faithful to this ideal. (Achille Cardinal Liénart, Bishop of Lille, *Le Monde*, May 12–13, 1963)

It is essential that the Church, which does not want to be rich, should be set free from the appearance of riches. The Church must appear as she is: the Mother of the poor, whose first care it is to give the bread of the body and the bread of the soul to her children, as John XXIII declared on September 11, 1962: "The Church is and wants to be the Church of all, and in particular the Church of the poor." She must direct those who have the necessities of life to the work of providing for those who still lack them. As bishops, we must keep in the forefront of our Council's preoccupations the problem of preaching the Gospel to the poor, of the apostolate among the workers. The present Council must be the opportunity of asserting this. (Pierre-Marie Paul Cardinal Gerlier, Archbishop of Lyons, quoted in *Equipes Enseignantes*, special number, 2e trimestre 1962–63, p. 89)

As a bishop, I cannot simplify everything overnight, but I must go on asking myself questions about the clothes that tradition makes me wear in liturgical ceremonies or elsewhere, on the marks of honour paid to me in the course of offices and in everyday life....

    I need hardly say too that I cannot fail to be concerned with the problem of honorific distinctions in the diocese. We shall be nominating canons for the next Feast of St. Vaast, but I know that many priests in the diocese look forward eagerly to the day when the majority of clergy will be in favour of abandoning a custom that goes back no further than the nineteenth century and belongs more to the spirit of the "world" than to the Spirit of Christ.

As priests, we must face, for example, the problem of the adornment of our churches. St. John Chrysostom several times sold sacred vessels to succour the poor….We need not imitate him too literally, but we must not be too ready to say that nothing is too fine or too costly for the glory of God, when two men out of three are dying of hunger. (Gérard-Maurice-Eugène Huyghe, Bishop of Arras, *Documentation Catholique*, March 3, 1963, col. 323–24)

Many bishops have already achieved a greater degree of poverty and simplicity in their dress. Why not go further, and apply the Gospel text, "not gold nor silver" literally to ourselves in the case of our episcopal insignia, and have them in base metal? Another real proof of the spirit of poverty would be the suppression of worldly and honorific titles bestowed on bishops. Why not give them back the title which expresses their first characteristic, fatherhood in the spirit: "Father"? Did not St. Peter say: "Do not lord it over those in your charge, but be examples to the flock"? (1 Peter 5:3).

Why retain, outside the church, genuflection as a mark of special respect? Still other simplifications, in liturgical ornament, style of life, etc., could be suggested. Certainly nothing is too beautiful for the liturgy, but the liturgy cannot justify the appearance of wealth in personal life.

The Pope recently reminded nuns throughout the world, shortly before the Council (July 7, 1962), that poverty is not easily reconciled with "ostentation in buildings or furnishings which have in some cases given rise to unfavorable comment." Why do not missions and dioceses take more care to keep their buildings, and especially their living quarters, down to a reasonable standard of comfort without over-refinement or extravagance? Progressive bishops have gone to the length of electing to live in humble accommodation in poor districts and converting their episcopal palaces into schools. It would be well if their example proved contagious!

Modern business equipment is essential if the overwhelming tasks of the apostolate are to be more speedily performed, and this includes bank accounts. But here again there is immense scope for the spirit of poverty; for example, if it is a question of transport, make the choice of a good working car, and never, whatever the rank to be upheld, of a deluxe model!

The Second Vatican Council is the first to meet when the Church is already poor, without temporal State, without political power for her papacy, but more radiant and more highly regarded than ever before. *Should not the body of bishops take the initiative by stripping itself voluntarily of all that still remains of external signs of wealthy of the temporal power that is now happily a thing of the past?* Nothing would bring home to the world more effectively the true nature of the kingdom and the Church. What *spiritual benefits* would the Holy Spirit not pour out on the whole Church if she made herself thus "poor in spirit," in conformity with the first Beatitude!

From actual poverty thus regained would flow a humility that would make her infinitely more responsive to the motions of the Holy Spirit, more open to approaches for unity, more receptive to the suffering of the world, and more generous in the service of the poor and of peace among men. (Georges-Louis Mercier, Bishop of Laghouat, quoted in *Equipes Ensiegnantes*, special number, 2e trimestre 1962–63, pp. 89–90)

"The Church and the poor: everywhere there is something to be done to make the Church really the church of all, and in particular the Church of the poor...." Poverty is a matter of life and death for the Church; without it she will lose the world of the workers. For the serious thing is that the working-class population, especially in some regions of Western

Europe, is escaping the Church. Those who are seeking the solution in this direction have my whole-hearted support. If anything is decided I shall be the first to put it into effect, to sacrifice what little I have. What is needed is a renewal of the Spirit, not of the Church moved by the Holy Spirit, but of men of the Church…who are not all saints. I implore God's grace and blessing for the good of the Church and the people. (Maximos V [George] Hakim, Melkite Patriarch of Antioch, quoted in *Equipes Enseignantes*, p. 87)

The various external signs and ceremonies that enhance the person of the bishop in particular made their appearance only during the course of the Church's history, more especially in the time of the Emperor Constantine, when the external honors to which the high officials of the Roman Empire might lay claim were specified and extended to the bishops. It is possible for the Church to conceive of herself without these external honorific distinctions. Where she faces persecution she must renounce them, and that does no harm to her inner life. (Josef Cardinal Frings, Archbishop of Cologne, *Lenten Pastoral Letter*, 1963)

The second of the Gospel values: *poverty and simplicity*. How many in the masses reproach the Church for her apparent wealth, the pomp of her ceremonies, her outward show, the place she seems to give to honors, money and "class" even in acts of worship! This is a real obstacle to the evangelization of the poor and the working masses who feel there is no place for them in the Church. In some parishes in France a real effort has begun to show the Church in her true aspect, poor and deprived in spite of appearances. But there is still much to be done in this direction. Moving appeals for poverty and simplicity have been made in the assemblies of the Council. They have been whole-heartedly echoed by the bishops. The Holy Father himself, in his allocution of September 11, said: "Confronted by the underdeveloped countries, the Church presents herself as she is and wants to be: the Church of all men, and in particular the Church of the poor." And the message of the Fathers in Council declared: "Our solicitude reaches out to the humblest, the poorest, the weakest. Like Christ, we are moved with compassion at the sight of the multitude suffering in hunger, misery, and ignorance." Consideration is being given to the creation of a permanent secretariat to study the great human and social problems, in particular the problems of the poor.

The third of the Gospel values: *the supremacy of love* over legalism in the Church. Too much emphasis on legalism, the result of seeing the Church above all as a society, risks making the obedience of the faithful to the "laws" of the Church into something purely external, passive and material. People go to mass on Sunday because the "laws" of the Church require it. They do not know why the Church requires it. They do not know that the Church requires it so that their souls may receive life. Laws are needed in every society, but the great law of the Gospel is the law of charity. The Church certainly is a juridical society, but she is also and above all a community of love. Her inner law is the law of the Holy Spirit, says St. Thomas, the Holy Spirit, the soul of the Mystical Body that is the Church, the Spirit of love who fills our hearts with charity; this law must be the life of all the Church's institutions. (Emile Maurice Guerry, Archbishop of Cambrai, *Pastoral Letter*, 1963)

How difficult it is for us poor bishops of the Church of Christ in the twentieth century to put across the message which at its beginning was steeped in the poverty of the incarnation, the manger, the cross, preached by a working man who lived his life of poverty without even a hole like the foxes, who washed the bare feet of the men he called his "friends," who used the familiar image of the lost goat. Today this message must go out to men living the bleak life of the proletariat, sixty-five per cent of them hungry, some existing in favellas, slums and shanty-towns; who call each other "comrade" and are accustomed to the incisive, direct speech of their leaders, to the sober lines of their sky-scrapers, their jet aircraft, and the shorts which are the review uniform of their generals. And we for our part have to deliver this message from the height of our marble altars and episcopal "palaces," in the incomprehensible baroque idiom of our pontifical masses, with their strange mitered ballet, in the still stranger circumlocutions of our ecclesiastical language; and we go out to meet our people clad in purple, in a car of the latest model or a first-class railway carriage, and our people come to us calling us "Your Eminence," and genuflecting to kiss the stone of our ring!

It is not easy to struggle free of all this weight of history and tradition. (Juan José Iriarte, Bishop of Reconquista, Argentina, *Le Monde*, June 1, 1963)

Because the Church is a form of Christ's presence in the world, she must reproduce Christ's image as perfectly as possible, and in her visible as well as her hidden life. The poverty that is the sign of the Incarnation must be the sign of the Church too.

All through history, customs have crept in, in ecclesiastical usage as well as in divine worship, which are inspired by worldly vanity rather than the simplicity and brotherhood of the Gospel. We have good grounds for thinking that the Council will in this sphere meet the aspirations of many of the clergy and the faithful....Already, for instance, the Fathers have adopted the principle of allowing no privileges to money in liturgical ceremonies, which should mean that the classes come together at funerals and marriages.

But here again, no reform can really bear fruit if Christians as a whole do not resolutely and wholeheartedly enter into the spirit which inspired it.

In short, the Church will find her true style of living, and will be the Church of the poor, only in the degree to which every Christian strives to live by Christ and, like him, to be "poor in spirit." (Louis-Jean-Frédéric Guyot, Bishop of Coutances and Avranches, *Lenten Pastoral Letter*, 1963, p. 16)

NOTES

I–1.
THE HIERARCHY AS SERVICE

1. St. Augustine had already said that the bishop is *servus servorum Dei, Epist.* 217 (*PL* 33, 378). We find the expression again in St. Gregory, but it is also in St. Benedict.

2. See the *Serm. tract.* 32 of the *Sermones inediti* published by D. G. Morin (*Miscell. Agostiniana*, vol. 1, Rome 1930, pp. 563–75), and St. Augustine's sermons on the anniversary of his own consecration as bishop, *Serm.* 339 and 340 (*PL* 38, 1480–4).

3. There is a vast literature on "Mirrors" and *De officiis*, less well-known when it deals with the clergy than with princes. The *De consideratione* of St. Bernard was widely read and extensively quoted. St. Bonaventure expressed his idea of the superior in a less famous work, *De sex aliis Seraphim* (*Opera*, vol. 8, pp. 131–51). Cf. Denys the Carthusian, *De vita et regimine praesulum* (*Opera*, vol. 37, pp. 11–57).

4. On this glory *which is from God* (not from men), cf. John 5:39–44; 7:16–18; 8:54. Christ's glory is the glory befitting an only begotten Son: 1:14.

5. Cf. John 7:39; 12:23–28; 13:31ff.; 17:1, 5.

6. See John 3:35, with the note in the *Jerusalem Bible*.

7. The verb *kurieuo* means "to be or become a lord, to act as a lord, to play the lord." *Katakurieuo* (see 1 Pet 5:3) adds to *kurieuo* a sense of making one's power felt, exercising dominion to one's own profit even to the detriment of others. The word *katexousiazousin* by

itself means no more than "to exercise power" (over one's subjects), but no doubt has here a similar nuance of dominion. Cf. 3 John 9, on Diotrephes, who loved to have the preeminence, *philoproteuon.*

8. See Isaiah 42:1 and the note in the *Jerusalem Bible* on this text.

9. In his commentary on Matt 20:25–28, Thomas Aquinas, whose roots in the Gospel becomes more apparent the better one knows him, propounds an example to himself: Can Christ, who allowed himself to be served (cf. Matt 4:11; John 12:2), himself be called *servus?* His answer is yes, for "servus dicitur qui accipitur in pretium: et ipse fecit se pretium et dedit se redemptionem pro multis." Cf. the Office of the Solemnity of the Body and Blood of Christ, *Pange lingua* ("quem in mundi pretium…"); *Verbum supernum* ("Se nascens dedit socium… se moriens in pretium…").

Cf. St. Bernard. In his comment on the theme of service by the angels, who exercise a pure *ministerium* for our benefit, he adds that Christ serves us by giving himself to us: "Non sic minister ille sublimior cunctis, sed et humilior universis, qui semetipsum obtulit sacrificium laudis, qui Patri offerens animam suam, nobis ministrat usque hodie carnem suam" (*Sermo 1 in Festo S. Michaelis,* n. 3, *PL* 183, 449).

10. Cf. 1 Cor 15:23–28: "But each in his own order: Christ the first fruits, then at his coming those who belong to Christ….For he must reign until he has put all his enemies under his feet….When all things are subjected to him, then the Son himself will also be subjected to the one who put all things in subjection under him, so that God may be all in all."

11. There are correspondences and connections between "As the Father has sent me, I also send you" (John 20:19ff., although the verbs used are not the same, cf. 4:38; 17:17–19), "As the Father has loved me, I also have loved you" (15:9; 17:18, 25; 13:34), the communication of the knowledge of the Father to the Son and from the Son to the disciples, with the "I know my own and my own know me, just as the Father knows me and I know the Father" (10:14–15), the glorification of the Father in the Son (13:31; 14:13), then of the Son, and so of the Father (15:8) in those he sends (17:1–5, 6, 8, 10), the mutual presence of the Father and the Son, of the Son and his disciples (14:20; 15:4), etc.

12. Rom 1:1; Phil 1:1; Gal 1:1; Titus 1:1. Servant of the faithful: 2 Cor 4:5; 1 Cor 9:19. Cf. for Epaphras, Col 4:12; for Timothy, 2 Tim 2:24.

13. Jas 1:1; 2 Pet 1:1; Jude 1.

14. See Rom 6:22; 1 Pet 2:16; Rev 1:1; 2:20; 7:3; 19:2, 5; 22:3, 6.

15. 1 Cor 7:10, 12, 17; 2 Cor 10:8; 2 Thess 3:9; Phlm 8.

16. Ibid.

17. Cf. the *Epistle of Barnabas*: "I will show you a few things, not as a teacher but as one of yourselves, whereby you shall rejoice in the present circumstances (I, 8); And this also I ask you, as being one of yourselves, and loving you individually and all together above my own life…. (IV, 6); And though wishing to write much, I am anxious to write not as a teacher but as your devoted slave" (IV, 9) (trans. *S.P.C.K. Texts for Students*, no. 14a, London: SPCK, 1923).

18. See 1 Cor 9, especially v. 15; 2 Cor 7:2ff.; 2 Thess 2:7. Cf. 2 Cor 9:7 and Acts 20:35 (the well-known saying: "It is more blessed to give than to receive").

19. See 2 Thess 3:7–9; cf. 1 Pet 5:3 ("examples to the flock").

20. See my paper, "La Casuistique de saint Paul," in *Sacerdoce et laïcat devant leurs tâches d'évangelisation et de civilisation* (Paris: Cerf, 1962), 65–90.

21. Thus, in St. Matthew's Gospel, 16:21–23 is followed by 16:26–27; the "If any want to become my followers" follows the confession of Peter (Matt 16:24; Luke 9:23); Matt 17:22–23 is followed by 18:1–4 (cf. Mark 9:30–36); Matt 20:17–19, followed by 20:20–8; James and John drink of the chalice. Matt 20:20ff.; Mark 10:35ff.

22. The apostle's sufferings: Col 1:24. Death, setting the seal on the apostolate for Paul: Phil 2:17–18; cf. 2 Cor 12:15; Acts 9:15–16; 20:24; 21:13. For the apostles to whom the liturgy ascribes the title of martyr: John 17:18–19; Heb 13:7.

23. In the Gospels, the word is almost always applied to Jesus, who "teaches" with authority (5 times), "pardons" with authority (4 times), "acts" with authority (7 times), "will judge" (twice). It is also used of God (3 times), the devil (5 times), earthly magistrates (9 times), the heavenly powers (13 times). In Revelation, it is used 19 times (for God, the Lamb, the satanic beasts). In eleven cases, the word has the weakened sense of permission, liberty (e.g. 1 Cor 8:9).

24. See, for example, Luke 1:2; Acts 6:4; 19:22; 20:24; 21:19; Rom 11:13; 12:7; 1 Cor 3:5; 12:5; 2 Cor 6:3; Eph 4:11; 1 Pet 4:11.

I–2.
HISTORICAL DEVELOPMENT OF AUTHORITY

1. John Henry Newman, "The Mission of St. Benedict," *Historical Sketches* (London: Basil Montagu Pickering, 1876), 417.

2. *Epist.* 66:8. At the time of writing, Cyprian was away from his community.

3. For example, the letter of Clement of Rome to the Church of Corinth. Eusebius says of a letter of Denys of Corinth, "It is addressed by him and by the Church he governed to Xystus and the Church of Rome" (*Hist. Eccl.*, VII. 9, 6).

4. Ignatius of Antioch, for example, connects the hierarchical and the community principles (*Magn,* VI and VII; *Smym.*, VIII), but insists on the hierarchical principle as the very condition of the community's existence (*Magn.*, III; XIII; *Trall.*, II–III, 1; *Philad.*, *superscription* and IV). For Clement, see especially *Cor.* XLIV and LXIII (hierarchical principle) and XXXIV. 7; XXXVII. 5 (community).

5. *Epist.* 14:4 ("nihil sine consilio vestro et sine consensu plebis mea privatim sentential gerere"). Cf. *Epist.* 34:4, 1; *Epist.* 32.

6. In St. Cyprian, *Epist.* 57:5. Warnings and signs had already been followed among the pagans when appointments to office were made. A similar practice is sometimes found in the Middle Ages. St. Bernard pays heed to them when deciding between Innocent II and Anacletus II, and Gratian lends his weight to the idea. It is God who controls the life of the Church.

7. Paulinus, *Vita Ambrosii*, c. 3, sect. 8.

8. Ambrose himself said he did not wish to be a conqueror but a physician: *De fide*, 1.11 (*PL* 16, 579). We know the famous passage of Augustine on Ambrose: "That man of God received me as a father and showed me an episcopal kindness on my change of home. And I began to love him, at first not as a teacher of the truth (which I utterly despaired of in your Church) but as a person who was kind to me" (*Suscepit me paterne ille homo Dei et peregrinationem meam satis episcopaliter dilexit. Et eum amare coepi primo quidem non tamquam doctorem veri, quod in Ecclesia tua prorsus desperabam, sed tamquam hominem benignum in me... Conf.* V. 13, 23 —PL 32, 717). For *episcopaliter*, we may refer to the distinction made by St. Jerome (*In Tit.*, c. 1,

v. 8—*PL* 26, 603) between the hospitality of a layperson who entertains a *few* persons, and that of a churchman, a bishop, who has a welcome for *all*.

9. *Reg.* V. 37; M.G.H., *Epp.*, I, p. 323—*PL* 77, 747 B.

10. *Summus igitur locus bene regitur, cum is qui praeest, vitiis potius quam fratribus dominator* in *Reg. Past.* II. 6 (*PL* 77, 36 C).

11. In a letter written in February 601 to Theoctista, the Emperor's sister, Gregory notes that the apostle Peter himself explained to the Church the reasons for his baptism of Cornelius: *Quaerelae fidelium non ex potestate, sed ex ratione, respondit, causam per ordinem exposuit* (*Reg.* XI, 27; M.G.H. *Epp.*, II, p. 293). This is the exact opposite of a remark made by an important member of the Curia: "Authority's proper characteristic is that it has not to give any reasons."

12. *Curandum quippe est, ut rectorem subditis et matrem pietas et patrem exhibeat discipline*, *Reg. Past.*, II. 6 (*PL* 77, 38 A).

13. This is the vocabulary used by St. Cyprian and St. Augustine. Later, the term was to be *praelati ecclesiae* (St. Thomas).

14. *Vobis sum epicopus, vobiscum christianus*. For this formula see *Sermo* 340.1 (*PL* 38, 1483).

15. *Qui praefuturus est omnibus, ab omnibus eligatur*. This is St. Leo's formula in *Epist.* 10.4 (*PL* 54, 628).

16. *Nullus invitis detur episcopus* This is the formula of Celestine I in *Epist.* 4, c. 5 (*PL* 50, 434). It occurs again in the Councils of Orleans (549) and Paris (557), and in Gratian's *Decretum*, C. 13 D., LXI (Friedberg, 231). There are similar formulae as early as 314—the Council of Ancyra, canon 18 (Bruns I. 69).

17. *Serm.* 335. 3 seq., and 356.2 seq. (*PL* 39, 1570 seq. and 1575 seq.). For St. Augustine, the acknowledgment of one's own weaknesses was demanded if one were to be able to admonish other people. Cf. *Contra Epist. Parmen.*, III. 5, 26 (*PL* 43, 103).

18. *Constitutum Sylvestri*, c. 3 (a document forged during the pontificate of Pope Symmacus, 498–514).

19. See Hinschius, *Kirchenrecht*, vol. I, p. 144 seq.; J. Gaudemet, op. cit., p. 156.

20. In 428, Pope Celestine I upbraided Honoratus abbot of Lerins, who had been appointed bishop of Arles, for introducing a special dress, namely, the tunic and belt. This was the monastic habit and an innovation. Hitherto, priests' dress was exactly the same as that of other men. Even in the celebration of the liturgy they merely wore *clean*

clothes. Celestine wrote to the bishops of the Narbonne province: "We should be distinguished from others, not by our dress but by our knowledge, by our conversation, not by our manner of life" (*Epist.* 4. 1, 2—*PL* 50, 431).

21. Hugo Rahner, *Servir dans l'Eglise, Ignace de Loyola et la Genèse des Exercices* (Paris: Editions l'Epi, 1959).

22. Mauro Capellari (Gregory XVI), in the opening address of his *Il trionfo della santa sede e della chiesa contro gli assalti de novatori respinti e combattuti colle stesse loro armi* (1799). In patristic terminology, the phrase would have been *rectores dominici gregis*—see Gelasius I, *Epist.* 6:2.

23. These words from Rev 19:16 are often used in this sense.

24. The idea of the Church as queen is frequent in iconography but is not so common in theological writings or official documents. Yet it is evident in the gradual change from the notion of Mother Church to that of the Church as *magistra* and *domina*, which is extremely common.

25. The word appears in the latter part of the eleventh century.

26. See my "L'ecclesiologie de saint Bernard," in *Saint Bernard theologien* (*Analecta Sacri Ordinis Cisterciensis*, 9, 1953), 164–5, 183.

27. *Filialiter et obedienter non obedio, contradico et rebello*— *Epist.* 128.

28. The ancient meaning of the word *magisterium* is "teaching, doctrine." In the Middle Ages, the word commonly indicates the situation or the activity of a master or, in a more general sense, authority to decide or to govern. Applied to the Church, the word sometimes has a meaning somewhat akin to the one it has today, for example, in Bernard de Fontcaude, *Contra Vallenses*, ch. 2, n. 4 (*PL* 204, 799 B, 1185+). However, *magisterium* in the sense of "the teaching Church" seems to be a modern usage.

29. Obedience becomes the fundamental virtue. See the bull *Exsurge*, which condemned Luther: *Nervum ecclesiasticae disciplinae, obedientiam scilicet, quae fons est et origo omnium virtutum* (Mansi, vol. 32, col. 1053).

30. Typical examples are Blessed John of Avila and St. Charles Borromeo.

31. Fourth Lateran Council (1215), can. 10.

32. Quoted by Roger Aubert, *Le Pontificat de Pie IX* (Paris: Bloud & Gay, 1952), 452.

33. Complaint of A. Loisy, *Mémoires pour servir à l'histoire religieuse de notre temps*, vol. 2 (Paris: E. Nourry, 1931), 368.

34. The letter of Clement to the Corinthians is a letter from the Roman community. Pius IX promulgated the constitutions of the Vatican under the heading *Pius, sacro approbante concilia*.

I–3.
THE CHRISTIAN CONCEPT OF AUTHORITY

1. See Ezek 34; Jer 23:1–6; John 10.

2. See Num 16:15; 1 Sam 12:3; Neh 5:14ff.; 1 Thess 2:9 (with the note in the *Jerusalem Bible*); 2 Thess 3:8; Phil 4:15.

3. It is told in the life of St. Bonaventure how, on the way to the General Chapter at Assisi, he was stopped by a simple friar who asked his help and consolation. The minister general gave him his full attention. To those who remonstrated with him, saying that he had better things to do, he replied, "I am a minister, a servant: he is my master…." St. Vincent de Paul often talked of "the poor, our masters…." When one is truly a servant, the other is the master and gives the orders; one does one's best to satisfy him.

4. Paul Broutin, *Mysterium Ecclesiae* (Paris: Orante, 1945), 255.

5. See my *Vaste monde ma paroisse: vérité et dimensions du salut* (Paris: Cerf, 1959), 56ff. English translation, *The Wide World My Parish: Salvation and Its Problems* (Baltimore: Helicon, 1961).

6. This is simply a summary of St. Thomas's entirely evangelical doctrine on the nature of the "new law" (which is the Gospel): *ST.*, Ia IIae, q. 106, a.1 and 2; q. 107, a.1, ad 3; q. 108, a.1; *Com. in Hebr.*, c.8, lect. 2; *De Ver.*, q. 17, a. 5.

7. See 1 Cor 12:27; Rom 12:5; 1 Cor 6:15; 12:12ff.; Eph 1:23; 4:16; 5:30; Col 1:24.

8. 1 Pet 4:10; Cf. Gal 6:1–2; Rom 15:14; 2 Cor 1:4; Col 3:16; 1 Thess 5:11, 14; 2 Thess 3:15; Heb 3:13; 10:24–25. Hugh of Saint Victor: *Unusquisque non sibi soli habet, etiam id quod solus habet* (*De sacrum*, 1. II, p. 2, c. 2; *PL* 176, 416); cf. St. Peter Damian, *Opusc.* "*Dominus vobiscum,*" c. 5–18 (*PL* 145, 235–46).

9. Gal 5:13; cf. 6:2; 1 Cor 9:19–23 ("all things to all men"); 2 Cor 4:5.

10. Georges Bernanos, *Les Enfants humilés: journal 1939–1940* (Paris: Gallimard, 1949), 36.

11. Lucien Laberthonnière, "Théorie de l'éducation," in *Essais de Philosophie religieuse* (Paris: P. Lethielleux, 1903), 261–62. The passage continues: "Those who command and those who obey have the same goal, and should be inspired by the same spirit. The only difference is that those who command have a greater responsibility; they are especially answerable for the others in the degree to which the others have been specially entrusted to them." For St. Thomas, see *ST*, IIa IIae, q. 104, a. 1 and 4.

12. Ministry of the word: Luke 1:2; Acts 6:4; 19:22; Rom 12:7; 2 Cor 5:18ff.; 2 Tim 4:5. Cf. the priestly service of the Gospel, Rom 15:16. The ministry of the Gospel becomes the ministry of justice, of the spirit, 2 Cor 3:7–9. For worship, the usual verbs are *latreuein* (Rom 12:1; cf. 2 Tim 1:3; Phil 3:3, and eschatologically, Rev 7:15; 22:3), although *latreuein* is also used of the service of the Gospel, Rom 1:9; and *leitourgein* (Acts 13:2), although this is applied to the service of faith (Phil 2:17; Rom 15:16) and collection (2 Cor 9:12).

13. Thus teaching is an ordained ministry (Acts 13:1; 1 Cor 12:28; Eph 4:11; 1 Tim 4:13; 2 Tim 1:11) but also a gift freely given to individuals (Rom 12:7). Prophecy is a ministry (Acts 13:1; 1 Cor 12:28; Eph 4:11) and a gift (Rom 12:6; 1 Cor 12:10; 13:2; 14:1ff., 29ff.). To be an evangelist is an order (Acts 21:8; Eph 4:11; 2 Tim 4:5; see also 1 Tim 4:14; 2 Tim 1:6) and a gift (Acts 8:4). Similarly, for exhortation (1 Tim 4:13, etc., on the one hand; Rom 12:8, on the other), speaking with tongues (Acts 2:14; 1 Cor 14:18, etc. on the one hand; 1 Cor 12:10, etc., on the other).

14. See, for example, St. Thomas, *IV Sent.*, d. 24, q. 1, a. 1, qa 1 (*Suppl.*, q. 34, a. 1, ad 1); *ST*, IIa IIae, q. 3, a. 2, ad 1 and 3; *In 2 Cor.*, c. 4, lect. 2.

15. Fr. L. Laberthonnière: "Those who are called to command in this world, as well as those who are compelled to obey, no longer consider themselves as holding a position of superiority, a transcendent right to impose on others; but as having a function to exercise, a duty to fulfil towards them—in short, to be of use, not to use them, *ministrare* and not *ministrari*. This is because all have to strive towards the same spiritual goal, which is to bring about the communion of souls in God,

and all must therefore practice the same duty of charity one towards another; so that in this perspective the distinction between those who command and those who obey has no meaning or scope except for the exterior and transitory order of this world." *Etudes sur Descartes*, vol. 2, p. 296 (quoted by L. Canet in the foreword to his edition of *La notion chrétienne de l'autorité* (Paris: J. Vrin, 1955), 40).

The passages of Fr. Laberthonnière collected by L. Canet in this book are inspired by profound thinking, which I have found stimulating. I feel, though, that his thinking falls short of the promise of his title, and so is not altogether satisfactory. It seems to me that Fr. Laberthonnière sometimes excludes, or at least pretermits or belittles, any authority other than that attractive form exercised in sacrifice of *self* (see p. 16, end of note; p. 17n1). All he sees is the moral aspect, or the aspect of the *education* of individuals, not the social aspect as such. He says, for example, of those who command, that they "have only a greater responsibility" (p. 34). This is dangerous, and may lead us to overlook the fact that their position of command gives them a title to responsibility other than the responsibility that every Christian has, and that this comprises authority in its strict sense. But it is true that essentially this authority gives them their place and order in the Christian condition, which consists entirely of service.

16. See Nikolaj Berdjaev, "The New Middle Ages," in *The End of Our Time* (London: Sheed & Ward, 1933) (although we reserve judgement on the position of the whole work): "Power is a duty and not a right, and power is just only if one claims it not in one's own name, or the name of one's people, but in the name of God—the name of truth." This passage expresses well the ethical aspect of the metaphysical argument that all power comes from God.

17. Tertullian, *De pudicitia*, 21, 6 (Oehler, p. 842). Cf. Origen, "The man who is called to the episcopate is not called to command, but to the service of the whole Church" (*In Isaiam*, hom. 6, 1; *In Mat.* comm. XVI, 8).

18. St. Bernard distinguishes between *dominium* and *ministerium* (*De officio episcopi*, c. 1, 3; *PL* 182, 812) or between *dominatus* and *cura, dominium* and *dispensations cura* (*Ep.* 14 to Honorius II: 182, 117; *Ep.* 117, 1, col. 281, "sanctae suae Ecclesiae ministros, non dominos").

19. *De perf. vitae spir.*, c. 16 and 24; IIa IIae, q. 185, a. 4; *Quodl.* I, q. 14, ad 2.

20. *De perf.*, c. 16 to 18; IIa IIae, q. 185, a. 1 and 4. St. Thomas makes effective use of the most topical New Testament texts.

21. The treatises of Bartholomew of the Martyrs and Louis of Granada were widely read. St. Francis de Sales said, of his consecration as bishop, "God took me away from myself to take me to himself and give me to the people, that I should no longer live save for him and for them."

22. Although we must of course note the context (a letter to Henry IV), it is impossible not to feel that these words of Gregory VII are much to be regretted: *Non ultra putet [Henricus] sanctam ecclesiam sibi subjectam ut ancillam, non praelatum ut dominam* (No longer shall Henry consider the holy church subject to him like a serving girl but as set over him like his lord) (*Reg.* IV, 3; ed. Caspar, p. 298).

23. Bellarmine and Sander (*De visibili Monarchia Ecclesiae*, Louvain, 1571) justify the use of torture by "Feed my sheep"!

24. In this sense, Sir 32:1 has often been quoted.

25. See my "Vie dans le monde et vie 'dans le Seigneur,'" in *Les voies du Dieu vivant* (Paris: Cerf, 1962), 359–66.

II–1.
THE INVASION OF LEGALISM

1. Letter to the bishops, dukes, and counts of Germany, September 3, 1076.

2. The analytical spirit of scholasticism also played its part, when methodical distinctions, which can be so necessary and productive, began to lead to separation or dissociation. Even the great Cajetan (d. 1534) considered that a priest may say his breviary during the Kyrie of the sung mass, *quoniam tunc non tarn missa quam missae sollemnitas agitur*, "because it is not so much a mass as it is a feast" (*De valore orationum dictarum ab audientibus missam in die festo: Opuscula*, Antwerp 1612, fol. 118ᵉ). This example comes at the end of scholasticism. Here is one from its beginning: as a sequel to the heresy of Berengarius, and because of the introduction of dialectics into theology, the exact moment of consecration in the Eucharist had to be determined. The canonist produced formulas of this kind: the words of the consecration are the *forma* or the *modus consecrandi*, the rest is *decor sacramenti*.

3. See "La casuistique de saint Paul," in *Sacerdoce et Laïcat* (Paris: Cerf, 1962), 65–89.

4. André N. Bertrand, *Témoins: Notes sur l'action religieuse du chef* (Vichy: Eclaireurs unionistes de France, 1942), 59, quoted in André Lalande, *Vocabulaire technique et critique de la Philosophie*, 8th ed. (Paris: Presses universitaires de France, 1960).

5. "Bull. d'Ecclésiologie," in *Revue des Sciences philosophiques et théologiques* 31 (1947): 77ff.: reproduced in *Sainte Eglise* (Paris: Cerf., 1963), 549ff.

II–2.
HOW THE CHURCH HAS ACQUIRED ITS APPEARANCE OF PRIVILEGE

1. See Eusebius, *Hist. Eccl.*, VII, 30, 9 (for the throne, but Paul of S. sought a good many other signs of authority as well!) and 30, 19, for the appeal to Aurelian (*Sources Chrétiennes* 41 [Paris: Cerf, 1955], 216, 219). In his commentary on Matt 16:25, Origen speaks of leaders of the people of God, especially in large towns, who would not suffer even the most authentic disciples of Jesus to address them on an equal footing.

2. Optatus of Milevis, III, 3; *PL* 11, 900 B.

3. The Donatists, on the other hand, who were certainly not models of all the virtues and were perfectly prepared, if not to use violence themselves, at least to use the support of their allies, rejected the situation that the peace of Constantine created, and claimed to be the Church of the poor; see my general introduction to *Oeuvres de saint Augustin: Traités antidonatistes* (Paris: Desclee, 1963), 37ff. and 35n2.

4. Eusebius, *Vita Constantini*, III, 21.

5. Evidence for this in: Origen, in 244ff., *Comm. in Mat.* XVII, 24 (GCS, Orig. Werke, X, p. 625); *In Jerem. hom.* 4, 3: "Once there were men of faith, when noble martyrdom was common…." Eusebius noted how a state of well-being, the result of peace and imperial favor, induced a condition of indolence in which internal divisions flourished (*Hist. Eccl.*, VIII, 1; *Sources Chrétiennes* 55 [Paris: Cerf, 1958], 3–6); St. Ambrose, *Exp. in Ps.* 118, *sermo* 11n21–22; St. Gregory Nazianus, *Carm.* II, 1, *De Seipso*, XI: *De vita sua* 20ff. (*PG*, 37, 1031);

St. Jerome, *Vita Malchi Monachi*, 1: "postquam ad christianos principes venerit, potentia quidem et divitiis maior, sed virtutibus minor
facta est [Ecclesia]" (*PL* 23, 55: c. 390); St. Augustine, *En. in Ps.* 7,
9 (*PL* 36, 103: "postquam in tanto culmine nomen coepit esse chris-
tianum, crevit hypcrisis, id est simulatio, eorum scilicet qui nomine
christiano malunt hominibus placere quam Deo…."); *Ps.* 30 *sermo* 2,
6 (col. 242–43).

6. See my article on "Le thème du 'don de la Loi' dans l'art
paléochrétien," in *Nouvelle Revue Théologique* 84 (1962): 915–33.

7. The myth was active in the East in the idea of Constantinople—the Second Rome—and then of Moscow—the Third Rome—
an idea that still influences the world today! In a more or less secular
form, it reappears to some extent in all the myths of unity of the Christian world, or just of the world.

8. Text in Karl Mirbt, *Quellen zur Geschichte des Papsttums*, no.
228 (Freiburg: Mohr, 1895), 107–12.

9. Ibid., no. 13.

10. Ibid., no. 14.

11. Ibid., nos. 14 and 16.

12. Ibid., no. 15.

13. Ibid., no. 17.

14. Ibid., no. 18.

15. A certain archbishop of Rouen said that he had a wife, not
as archbishop of Rouen, but as count of Evreux. Of course, this exceptional case was contrary to anything said by the pope or synods.

16. There is no comparison between this and the retinues of the
feudal bishops of the Middle Ages, especially of the waning Middle
Ages. Here are some figures: at the Third Lateran Council (1179), prelates arrived with 20 to 30 horses; at the Council of Constance (1414–
18), the archbishop of Mainz had a retinue of 452, and the archbishop
of Salzburg, 260; at the Council of Trent (1545–63), Cardinal Ercole
Gonzaga had a retinue of 160, and Cardinal Alexander Farnèse (the
future Paul III) had 360 servants, but the average per prelate was nine.

17. Kissing the hand, genuflection; for popes, kissing the feet
(the old *proskunesis* of Byzantium, implying prostration), censing.

18. Gregory VII, *Dict.* 8; ed. Caspar, *Reg.*, p. 204.

19. This is what St. Peter Damian, himself a cardinal, says of the
College of Cardinals: *Romana Ecclesia, quae sedes est Apostolorum,
antiquam debet imitari Curiam Romanorum*: "The Roman Church,

which is the seat of the Apostles, should imitate the old Roman Senate" (*Opusc.* 31, *Contra philargyrium*, c. 7 (*PL* 145, 540).

20. See my paper, "L'ecclésiologie de saint Bernard," in *Saint Bernard théoligien: Anal. S. Ord. Cisterc.*, 9 (1953), pp. 136–90.

21. St. Bernard, *De Consideratione*, IV, 3, 6 (*PL* 182, 776 A).

22. *Tract. de moribus et off. episc.*, 2, 4 (*PL* 182, 813B).

23. *In Cant. sermo* 77, 1 (*PL* 183, 1155D–1156A).

24. *Tr. de moribus et off. episc.*, 9, 36 (182, 832 CD). The ring was widely used at the end of the twelfth century, but the adoption or concession of *pontificalia* for abbots reached its peak in the fourteenth.

25. *Est républicain* of January 5, 1959: "Noon on January 8—a historic moment: de Gaulle will be *consecrated* President of the Republic to the sound of a 101-gun salute."

26. Chateaubriand, art. of July 5, 1824, quoted in *Mémoires d'outre-tombe*, 3ᵉ partie, 2ᵉ époque, 1. VI, para. 8: "Time has reduced this monarchy to its reality. The age of fictions is over for politics; there can no longer be a government based on adoration, worship, and mystery: everyone knows his rights, nothing is possible beyond the boundaries of reason, and everything—even favor, that last illusion of absolute monarchies—is weighed and assessed today."

27. *Chronicle of Nestor.*